ORGANIZING FOR
SUICIDE PREVENTION

ORGANIZING FOR SUICIDE PREVENTION

A Case Study at the Golden Gate Bridge

Jennifer Lewis, Ph.D., LCSW
University of Southern California

and Paul Muller
Bridge Rail Foundation

SAN DIEGO

Bassim Hamadeh, CEO and Publisher
Amy Smith, Senior Project Editor
Casey Hands, Production Editor
Jess Estrella, Senior Graphic Designer
Stephanie Kohl, Licensing Coordinator
Natalie Piccotti, Director of Marketing
Kassie Graves, Vice President of Editorial
Jamie Giganti, Director of Academic Publishing

cognella® | ACADEMIC PUBLISHING
3970 Sorrento Valley Blvd., Ste. 500, San Diego, CA 92121

CONTENTS

INTRODUCTION

The terms *Suicide Prevention* and *Organizing* are not often seen together. Generally, when we hear of suicide prevention, we think of clinical interventions, crisis counseling, or warning signs that allow people to intervene with family or friends. These approaches are all important for prevention and absolutely necessary in many circumstances. Yet, one of the most effective suicide prevention activities requires no appointment, no call to a crisis line, and no special training. This activity is a very simple, straightforward concept—restricting easy access to lethal means. This approach is in the process of being employed in suicide "hotspots" around the country, most notably at the Golden Gate Bridge in San Francisco, California, in an attempt to end a long and tragic history of individuals jumping from the bridge to their death.

Our story is in three parts:

1. How a group of advocates grew and sustained a coalition of families touched by suicide, prevention supporters, health professionals, and other interested parties into a successful campaign for a suicide prevention structure at the Golden Gate Bridge.

2. What the research into suicide prevention and life-saving interventions has told us over the last 40 years.

3. How you—the reader, student, or community organizer—might approach a public campaign to address a suicide problem or other suicide-related mental health issue in your community.

Quite simply, our view is that social workers, mental health clinicians, and advocates must become adept at addressing suicide prevention, organizing allies, communicating with supporters and the public, and influencing policy makers to take the actions needed to eliminate preventable deaths. Specifically, how restricting access to lethal means will reduce suicides and that this approach can be applied to a wide variety of potentially suicidal situations.

Some sections of the book may be more appropriate and relevant for undergraduate or graduate social work macro courses focused on communities and organizations. The section on explaining how to evaluate community-level interventions could be useful in program evaluations or research courses. Community organizations or members may find the book helpful for training staff or individuals responsible for developing collaborative partnerships and taking action on the public stage. Finally, the chapter on clinical interventions may be useful for program administrators and clinicians alike. Social workers need to have the knowledge and skills to impact the problem on a micro, mezzo, and macro practice level. Much of what we report here can be applied to other projects addressing a wide range of social ills advocates may encounter on a daily basis.

If you or anyone you know is struggling with thoughts of suicide, please call the suicide prevention hotline at 1-800-273-8255. As of July 2022, you can simply dial 988.

Suicide at the Golden Gate Bridge

FIGURE 1.1 The Golden Gate as it was before the bridge.

M any thought it was a daft idea to construct a bridge across the Golden Gate Strait, a narrow pinch of land separating San Francisco Bay from the Pacific Ocean. Tides in the area are cold and swift, winds are strong, and the fog is frequent. Such straits are often of strategic importance, as was the Golden Gate with military installations dating to the period of Spanish rule. Indeed, there was formal resistance to bridge construction from the U.S. Navy, who feared an enemy might attempt to destroy any bridge across the Gate, thereby closing the harbor and trapping American warships in the bay. However, the politics aligned, the military cooperated, the state legislature created a special district to manage the bridge, and the financing was arranged to build it. The Golden Gate Bridge opened in 1937 during the Great Depression. Once opened, the bridge became an international symbol, engineering wonder, and popular hit with locals and tourists from around the globe. Yet, within the first 18 months, the bridge—with sidewalks and a short railing along its eastern and western edges—was the site of eleven suicides, creating a call for a suicide barrier. The first to advocate for some form of a barrier were the first responders, the cops on the beat—in this case, the California Highway Patrol. No action was taken.

A Suicide Hotspot

Over the next 6 decades, the deaths continued to mount. Meanwhile, there were studies, drawings, press exposés, and hearings relating to the issue, but no meaningful changes were made. Every conceivable reason was put forward for not taking action. Some claimed the engineering was too much of a challenge on a dynamic suspension bridge. Others insisted the iconic nature of the bridge design should remain untouched. Still others were concerned about the cost, or the simple fact that no money was budgeted to address the issue. In addition, many people argued that a suicide barrier would not work at all. A popular belief was that suicidal individuals impeded at the bridge would simply find other lethal means—another bridge, a gun, or pills.

Over the years, interest in suicide prevention at the Golden Gate would peak—as it might after the death of a well-known individual—but that interest would quickly fade. Yet the death toll continued to rise. There were occasional incidents of outrage as well, such as when a radio DJ offered a prize for the person who became jumper #1,000. Even as the suicides continued, not all of the deaths were properly counted. Strong currents, along with rising and ebbing tides, push through the narrow Golden Gate and greatly challenged the recovery work. Likewise, limited visibility caused by dense fog can both obscure a jump from the bridge and hamper search-and-rescue efforts by the Coast Guard and other first responders. Some who jump are quickly washed out to sea, not to be counted unless family members secure additional investigation or a body is subsequently found and identified. Still, by the close of 2016, more than 1,600 suicides were officially recorded, and the 5-year average annual number of deaths reached 35.

Very quickly, the suicide problem at the Gate had become well known and almost an accepted part of life and death in the Bay Area. Of course, not all were willing to accept this communal shrug at ongoing deaths. The 1960s saw psychiatrists and other physicians begin a concerted push for a barrier. In the 1970s, faith communities led an effort. Their work featured the coordinated ringing of church bells throughout San Francisco to call attention to the ongoing suicide deaths at the bridge. These efforts created some public interest but only got as far as the drawing board. In response, the Bridge District architect did produce multiple versions of suicide barrier designs, but the concepts went no further.

Local suicide prevention agencies joined together in the 1990s to fight for an end to suicides at the bridge. With intense effort and many hours of back-and-forth negotiations, their push for a suicide barrier also came up short. Instead, a compromise that split advocates was reached, whereby the Bridge District agreed to install phones on the bridge linked to suicide prevention hotlines and produce a sample barrier to gauge public reaction. The advocacy work ended with this compromise, but a great deal had been done to push the effort forward. Allies were identified among members of the independent Bridge District board of directors; the issue was again brought forward and put before the public; and supporters of a barrier learned some important lessons. Yet, for all those benefits, families continued to lose loved ones. The issue was not treated as the life-and-death matter that it was. Except by first responders, there was no urgent effort to stop the deaths.

Meanwhile, these first responders continued to be the last defense against the ongoing suicides. Bridge District patrol officers, union iron-workers, and the California Highway Patrol gained increased experience in talking people back over the short rail of the bridge. Yet, despite yearly fluctuations, the death toll continued to rise. By the end of the 20th century, San Francisco's most iconic landmark was the busiest single site for suicide on the planet. The Golden Gate Bridge became the very definition of a "suicide hotspot."

For years, the Bridge District tried to keep the suicide story quiet. In fact, an official policy was enacted on December 22, 1983, that restricted release of any information about suicide deaths without the prior approval of the Bridge District general manager. Later, the publication of suicide reporting press guidelines by national suicide prevention organizations was used as further justification by the Bridge District to obscure the death toll. This intentional fogging was so effective that the public was largely unaware of the severity of the problem. Even long-term Bridge District board members were not fully informed of the high annual death toll.

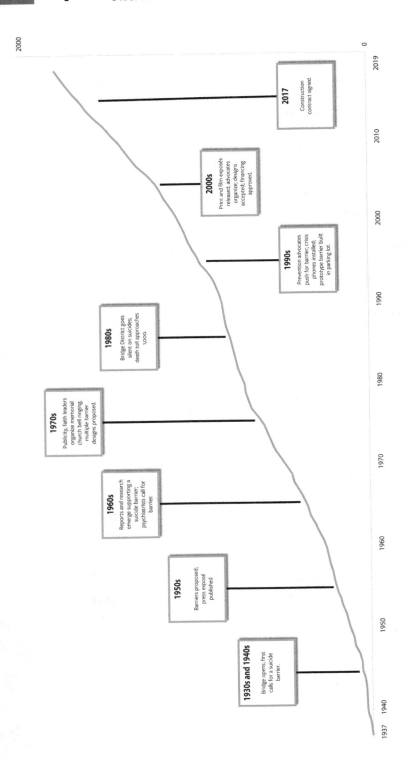

FIGURE 1.2 Timeline: Deaths and Decisions.

Data sources: Years 1937–1999, The Final Leap: Suicide on the Golden Gate Bridge, by John Bateson, University of California Press, 2012. Years 2000–2017, Golden Gate Bridge District. To include deaths where the remains were not recovered, we calculated the ratio of such deaths to known deaths from 2000 through 2017 and applied it to previous years. The result is a more accurate, but still incomplete, count.

One suicide that did break through this intentional fog was of a 14-year-old girl from Santa Rosa, a city 50 miles north of the bridge. Not yet of driving age, Marissa Imrie took a cab across the bridge, paid the driver, walked back along the pedestrian sidewalk, climbed the short railing, and jumped to her death. Typically, the district would take little official notice; however, Marissa's mother, Renee Milligan, was not satisfied with mere sympathy and condolences. She took the Bridge District to court. Whereas the lawsuit was unsuccessful, the district board and staff leadership were forced to take notice. Additionally, the ongoing suicide problem was a topic of quiet discussion, frustration, and sometimes anger among the Bridge District staff. Patrol officers and maintenance crews on the bridge were often the first to see or react to a suicide attempt that resulted in a jump. Likewise, the horror of bridge suicides was a regular experience for California Highway Patrol officers, U.S. Coast Guard personnel, San Francisco police and firefighters, and an untold number of tourists who witnessed a suicide while on a stroll across the bridge.

A Note on Language

The term *suicide hotspot* has two possible meanings:

1. A geographical area with a relatively high rate of suicide among its resident population (e.g., a town, borough, county, or country); or

2. A specific, usually public, site that is frequently used as a location for suicide and which provides either means or opportunity for suicide (e.g., a particular bridge from which individuals frequently jump to their deaths).

Many well-known locations throughout the world have become associated with suicidal acts. These locations include both manmade structures and natural sites, some of which have iconic status or significance. The Golden Gate Bridge, the Sydney Harbour Bridge, the Nanjing Yangtse River Bridge, the Empire State Building, and Niagara Falls have been among the top suicide sites worldwide. Such places seem to act as magnets, drawing suicidal individuals to them. These types of places are high risk because they provide opportunities for suicide by jumping from a height. Other types of high-risk environments include situations in which one can place themselves in front of a moving vehicle or other methods, such as car exhaust poisoning.

Exposed

Against this backdrop, the *New Yorker* published a classic journalistic exposé of the suicide problem at the Golden Gate.[1] The article triggered two events that would set the stage for approval of the needed suicide prevention structure at the bridge. The first of these was the production of Eric Steel's documentary *The Bridge*. The film captures most of the suicide deaths at the Golden Gate Bridge in 2004 and includes many of the personal and family stories behind the bridge jumps.[2] Kevin Hines's story of his jump and subsequent survival is recounted in the film. While Steel was filming, the Psychiatric Foundation of Northern California (PFNC) launched a new advocacy effort. Foundation head Mel Blaustein, MD, had read the *New Yorker* article. Like many in the local mental health community, he had lost patients to bridge jumps. Disagreements with PFNC's strategy and approach would later lead to the launch of the nonprofit organization Bridge Rail Foundation.

Who Is in Charge?

At the start of any advocacy project, the first question to confront is *Who are we dealing with?* California's transportation agency, CalTrans, manages almost every major bridge in the state. The exception is the Golden Gate, which is run by an independent board of directors appointed in a special district (Bridge District), authorized by the state legislature in 1928.[3] Directors are appointed by the board of supervisors in each of the district's six counties. The district is an odd one, in that it is only partially in the Bay Area. The original plan was to include the entire north coast of California—from San Francisco to the Oregon border. However, in the election to create the district, the people of Humboldt County refused to join, while the county further north, Del Norte, went along with the plan and joined the new district. Del Norte County is 350

---

1   Friend, T. (2003). JUMPERS. (Golden Gate Bridge as suicide magnet). The *New Yorker, 79*(30).

2   Steel, E. [YouTube Movies]. (2015). *The Bridge* [Video]. YouTube. https://www.youtube.com/watch?v=9l8PqnTy7Y4

3   Golden Gate Bridge, Highway and Transportation District. (2020). *Special district formed.* https://www.goldengate.org/bridge/history-research/bridge-construction/special-district-formed/

miles north of the Golden Gate. The result is a noncontiguous six-county governing agency with representation from each county. San Francisco has 9 of the seats on the 19-person board, followed by Marin (4), Sonoma (3), Napa (1), Mendocino (1), and Del Norte (1) counties.

FIGURE 1.3 The Golden Gate Bridge emerging from a bank of fog.

The Bridge District board is composed of county supervisors, city officials, and county supervisor-appointed citizens, bringing together a mixture of elected officials and appointed representatives. The Bridge District board therefore includes a number of local politicians, most fairly early in their respective political careers. Some, no doubt, imagine this career will eventually lead to the White House. That has yet to happen, but during the decades of effort to end the suicides at the bridge, various veterans of the district governing board moved upstream to the State Assembly, State Senate, and Congress.

This network of legally responsible board members and influential former board members was not the whole structure. In addition, the Bridge District was heavily dependent on the regional transportation planning agency, the Metropolitan Transportation Commission (MTC), which had control of the flow of federal funds for many of its transportation projects. Moreover, powerful San Francisco politicians would often insert themselves into Bridge District affairs. The city's mayors, many themselves eager for a higher office, wanted a say in what happened at the bridge. California's current governor, Gavin Newsom, was San Francisco's mayor during much of the advocacy work. Throughout this period, the bridge itself was partially in the congressional district of speaker of the U.S. House of Representatives, or minority leader Nancy Pelosi. In fact, from the 2003 publication of the *New Yorker* article through 2016, both of California's U.S. senators, Dianne Feinstein and Barbara Boxer, were former Bridge District board members.

Also in the mix of influence was a generous collection of advocacy groups with interests in the bridge because of its architectural heritage, ever-rising bridge tolls, access for bicycle riders, impact on the tourist economy, environmental concerns, labor and employment issues, and traffic safety, among other issues. Further, as an international landmark, anything that happened at the Golden Gate Bridge generated a great deal of press interest.

Although the district was formed to build the bridge and manage its finances and operation, this limited-purpose district began to see the need to grow or die. Therefore, in 1969, the district approached the legislature to expand its role with the additions of a bus service and a ferry system. The district's buses now serve San Francisco, Marin, Sonoma, and parts of western Contra Costa County. District ferries dock in San Francisco and Marin. This additional mission required a name change, so the district officially became the Golden Gate Bridge, Highway, and Transportation District. Most people in the Bay Area still refer to it as the "Bridge District," a tradition we have followed in this book.

Special districts similar to the Golden Gate tend to operate in obscurity. The public knows little of them, and their work is often of pale interest to the larger audiences served by mass media. However, the iconic nature of the Golden Gate Bridge makes the district much more visible and attracts a natural public following. For example, when the district has found occasion to raise bridge tolls, it has historically triggered a wave of publicity and consternation about the district, including how it is run and who is doing the running. As a highly visible and occasionally controversial public entity, the Bridge District was often an easy story for an ambitious cub reporter or an in-depth analysis from an experienced journalist. Likewise, it was easy prey for a cranky columnist or clever cartoonist.

All this complexity and public attention did not mean that power and influence in the district were too diffuse to function. In fact, the attention served to concentrate power at the center. Who could be in position to corral all these diverse influences and keep the operation humming along, protect the politicians from the negative effects of a toll increase or any other controversial effort, and ensure they were given credit in any positive publicity that might be generated? Who would keep the bridge open by denying access for promotional antics such as a march of the Budweiser® Clydesdale horses? Who would protect the traffic flow from protesting movie actors? And with a board that would not act, who could keep the suicide problem quiet while the lethal access remained? Suicide prevention advocates knew the answer to all these questions was simple—the staff.

G. GORDON KHAN: Obsessed with strategies to extract ever-escalating tolls from helpless Golden Gate Bridge commuters.

FIGURE 1.4 Phil Frank created this character to represent the Bridge District in a regular feature published in the *San Francisco Chronicle*. The bridge was always an easy target when commuter tolls were raised, while the *Chronicle's* journalists, columnists, and editorial writers continued to report on the increasing suicide deaths.

Early Efforts

The PFNC was fully aware that a successful campaign needed to include all of the various decision makers involved with the Golden Gate Bridge, so it moved to set its first meetings with Bridge District staff in 2004. At the time, Celia Kupersmith was the general manager at the Bridge District, a position that led the staff and reported directly to the board. Kupersmith turned down the foundation's request for a meeting. The foundation was referred to the public affairs director, Mary Currie, who agreed and organized a group of senior staffers to meet with them. Thus, several of the PFNC's task force members—including chair Mel Blaustein, MD, Jerry Motto, MD, Eve Meyer, head of SF Suicide Prevention, the foundation's executive director Janice Taggart, and consultant Paul Muller—gathered at Bridge District headquarters. They sat down with the district's public affairs manager Currie, bridge manager Kary Witt, and chief engineer Denis Mulligan. The meeting produced no commitments, and task force members in attendance left frustrated that no clear direction toward a solution was proposed. Likewise, there was little sense of urgency expressed to the advocates. However, the chief engineer was confident that a workable—though complex—solution could be designed. This assertion was a significant departure from the position represented by previous district engineers. In the past they had pointed to concerns about the load capacity of the bridge, the need for wind tunnel testing on any proposed structure, and the lack of funding to even explore their concerns, much less finance construction.

In spite of this frustrating first meeting, the PFNC proceeded; additional supporters were recruited, and brochures, PowerPoint® presentations, and posters were produced. A speaking program was organized as well. Task force members also cooperated with and supported a *San Francisco Chronicle* effort that produced a dramatic, week-long front-page report on the ongoing suicide problem. Likewise, task force members quietly cooperated with Steel's project as he was filming.

Things were well underway but concerns with both leadership and direction for the effort soon surfaced. Meetings with survivor family members frustrated some because they were not action oriented and offered a very limited role for these advocates. Eventually, this would lead to the organization of the nonprofit Bridge Rail Foundation (BRF), which would push for a suicide prevention structure at the Golden Gate for more than 10 years. Throughout the effort, Bridge Rail kept to a simple mission—stop the suicides at the Golden Gate Bridge. To reach this goal, the foundation employed a strategy best summarized in three words: organize, communicate, and persist. Each of these strategies will be explored in subsequent chapters.

The culmination of all these efforts and sacrifices by many who had lost friends and family members to suicide was a advocacy program that stayed active over the 12 years of planning, testing, engineering, and funding efforts. Advocates had persisted where others had been pushed aside. The final vote to award a construction contract for the suicide deterrent net passed in December of 2016—on a motion by bridge director John Moylan, whose grandson had recently died in a jump from the bridge. Support for Moylan's motion at the District Board meeting was unanimous.

For a more complete telling of the bridge suicide stories and the impact of these deaths on families, see *The Final Leap: Suicide on the Golden Gate Bridge* by John Bateson, University of California Press, 2012.

Likewise, for an interesting history of the Bridge District, its special-interest behavior, and impact on regional transportation, see *Paying the Toll: Local Power, Regional Politics, and the Golden Gate Bridge*, University of Pennsylvania Press, Paperback, December 18, 2013, by Louise Nelson Dyble.

FIGURE 1.5 Celebrating the official launch of construction, Bridge Rail board members and volunteers join with Denis Mulligan, general manager of the Bridge District, and then House minority leader Nancy Pelosi.

Timeline: Deaths and Decisions

1930s–1940s

	Golden Gate Bridge opens in May.
1937	Harold Wobber is the first suicide from the bridge in August.
1939	California Highway Patrol requests action to stop suicides.
1945	Following the death of a 5-year-old girl, debate on a suicide barrier appears in the *San Francisco Chronicle* letters to the editor August through November.

1950s

1951	Scores of Sunday drivers said to witness a suicide in July.
1953	Bridge director proposes Suicide Prevention Patrol or taller fencing.

1955	In January, engineering consultants tell the bridge director there is no sure way to stop suicides. At February board meeting, bridge board considers raising the railing or adding barbwire to stop suicides.
1957	TV monitor system proposed to stop suicides and monitor traffic.
1959	For 3 days in April, the *San Francisco Chronicle* runs front-page stories on the bridge suicide problem.

1960s

1962	Bridge is 25 years old in May, and the *Chronicle* notes, "No one knows how many melancholy beings have leaped from her side into oblivion, but the official toll is now 224."
1964	Bridge fence no answer to suicide problem, local psychiatrist argues in October.
1965	First report of Richard Seiden's detailed analysis of bridge suicides issued in March. To curb suicides, bridge general manager James Adams closes sidewalk from 6 p.m. to 8 a.m. Local politicians furious. Closed-circuit TV proposal submitted.
1968	Security Committee of the Bridge District votes to support a suicide barrier in April.
1969	A November seminar between San Francisco Suicide Prevention and the Bridge District recommends a 7-ft. fence bolted to the bridge.

1970s

1971	Bridge architects asked to design suicide prevention railings.
1973	In April, Bridge District votes 12–6 to order wind tunnel testing for a suicide barrier. The *San Francisco Chronicle* reports suicide #500.
1974	Bridge District engineer says design for the suicide barrier will not prevent all suicides, calls for redesign. In August, church bells ring throughout the Bay Area in commemoration of suicides from the bridge.
1975	Bridge District committee drops plans for a suicide barrier in April.

1976	In October, a boatload of tourists on the bay witness a suicide from the bridge.
	In August, a proposal for a suicide deterrent railing is made at the district.
1978	In the winter, Richard Seiden's research is published: of 515 suicide attempters removed from the bridge, only 25 subsequently die by suicide.

1980s

1983	Bridge District goes silent on suicide deaths.
1987	The Golden Gate Bridge is 50 years old, and the reported suicide count nears 1,000.

1990s

	Suicide prevention advocates launch push for a barrier.
1993	Phones connected to suicide prevention crisis lines installed on bridge.
	Bridge replaces 6,500 feet of rusted short railing with new short railing.
1998	In response to suicide prevention advocates, a prototype barrier installed in Bridge District parking lot.

2000s

2003	*New Yorker* article published in October.
	Film *The Bridge* captures most 2004 suicides from the Golden Gate.
2004	Psychiatric Foundation Task Force begins to push for a barrier.
	Reacting to news of *The Bridge,* Golden Gate Bridge District calls a hearing. Before many family and friends of bridge suicide victims, the district votes to request preliminary design and testing of suicide barrier options.
2005	UC–Berkeley engineering students release three design proposals for bridge suicide prevention.
	The *San Francisco Chronicle* publishes front-page articles on the suicide problem and the bridge on 5 successive days.
	Kevin Hines begins a national speaking program on suicide, survival, and the problem at the Golden Gate.

2006	Bridge Rail Foundation formally organized; Dave Hull elected president.
2007	Marin County coroner and Bridge Rail board member Ken Holmes releases detailed demographic study of bridge suicides. The *Los Angeles Times* quotes him saying, "I'm tired of the carnage, the public needs to know these needless deaths continue at an alarming rate."
2008	Suicide deterrent net is the preferred design, passes early testing. Bridge Rail Foundation organizes presentations for a district hearing that approves seeking funding for next planning steps and EIR.
2010	With EIR complete, the Bridge District agrees to proceed with the net as planned in February. Metropolitan Transportation Commission releases funds for engineering work on the suicide deterrent net in July. In September, Bridge Rail cosponsors a "Please Don't Jump" event to advocate for the net.
2012	May marks the 75th anniversary of the bridge opening. Bridge Rail exhibit at the celebration displays 1,558 pairs of shoes to represent suicide victims to date; story goes national.
2017	Contract signed for construction of suicide deterrent net in January.

Image Credits

2

Evaluate the Landscape

At the start of any advocacy project, proponents should have a solid understanding of the issues at hand. In this case, when advocating for suicide prevention, social workers and supporters need to be knowledgeable about the definition of suicide, national suicide data and trends in suicidal means, and high-risk groups in order to position themselves in relation to the national epidemic.

The Wide Reach of Suicide

For the sake of providing a clear definition, suicide—also referred to as self-directed violence—is death caused by injuring oneself with the intent to die.[1] A suicide attempt, on the other hand, is when someone harms themselves with the intent to end their life but does not subsequently die. According to the World Health Organization, almost 800,000 people die by suicide every year, which accounts for one person every 40 seconds.[2] Many more attempt suicide. There are indications that for each adult who dies by suicide, there may be more than 20 others who attempt it.

---

[1] Crosby, A. E., Ortega, L., & Melanson, C. (2011). Self-directed violence surveillance: Uniform definitions and recommended data elements (Version 1.0). Centers for Disease Control and Prevention, National Center for Injury Prevention and Control.

[2] World Health Organization. (2020). Suicide data. https://www.who.int/mental_health/prevention/suicide/suicideprevent/en/

Suicide isn't a problem isolated to one group, demographic, or region, but rather affects all walks of life to varying degrees. For instance, globally, suicide is the second leading cause of death among 15- to 29-year-olds, and 79% of suicides occurred in low- and middle-income countries in 2016. Further, suicide accounted for 1.4% of all deaths worldwide, making it the 18th leading cause of death in 2016.

FIGURE 2.1 Multiple police agencies respond to a potential suicide. Here, CHP officer Kevin Briggs speaks with Kevin Berthia, who is precariously close to a fatal jump. Briggs developed a relaxed, almost conversational tone when he approached a potential bridge suicide. Note that he has removed his helmet and adopted a casual forward-leaning stance while speaking with Berthia. Demographics reveal that Golden Gate suicides occur with a younger population than national statistics might predict. Likewise, African Americans represent 4.2% of the Golden Gate suicides, according to a 15-year study of coroner's records released by the Bridge Rail Foundation. The crisis pictured here was resolved when Berthia came back over the short rail.

Kevin Briggs later retired after talking over 200 individuals back from the brink at the bridge. He now teaches crisis response to other police. Kevin Berthia has become a suicide prevention advocate and speaks of his experience around the country. Police agencies, including the California Highway Patrol and uniformed Golden Gate Bridge patrol officers, stop over 150 people per year who are suspected of a suicide attempt. Yet the number of suicide deaths from the bridge continued to increase—to average over 30 per year from 2010 through 2019.

Suicide in the United States is a large and growing public health problem as well, positioned as the 10th leading cause of death. In 2017, it was responsible for nearly 47,173 deaths in the United States. On average, 129 Americans died by suicide each day. In 2017, there was an estimated 1.4 million Americans who attempted suicide.[3] According to the Centers for Disease Control and Prevention (CDC), the suicide rate in the United States has increased steadily since the turn of the millennium. Suicide rates are calculated as the number of deaths per 100,000 people, and between 2000 and 2006, the rate increased by about 1% every year. Over the next decade, from 2006 to 2017, the rate doubled to a 2% increase every year.[4]

The worsening state of suicide sits in stark contrast to improvements in other public health arenas, such as vaccines against polio and other preventable diseases, tobacco use, death from heart disease, early detection of cancer, treatment for HIV, early childhood health and nutrition, and oral health through fluoridation of drinking water.[5] This deviation of increased suicides in the face of advances in overall general health makes it clear that the problem of suicide is not going to go away on its own.

Suicide Rates and Demographic Considerations

According to data from the Surgeon General's Report,[6] suicide is a problem affecting all age groups. In the United States, suicide is the second leading cause of death for people 10–34 years old, the fourth leading cause among people 35–54 years old, and the eighth leading cause among people 55–64 years old. In 2016, the highest suicide rate was among adults between 45 and 54 years old. For every 100,000 individuals, there were 19.72 deaths. The second highest rate (18.98) occurred in those 85 years or older. Younger groups have consistently tended to have lower

3   American Foundation for Suicide Prevention. (2020). Suicide statistics. https://afsp.org/suicide-statistics/

4   National Center for Injury Prevention and Control. (2018, June 7). Suicide rising across the US: More than a mental health concern. Center for Disease Control and Prevention. https://www.cdc.gov/vitalsigns/suicide/index.html

5   Research America. (n.d.). Public health milestones. https://www.researchamerica.org/advocacy-action/public-health-thank-you-day/public-health-milestones

6   U.S. Department of Health and Human Services (HHS) Office of the Surgeon General and National Action Alliance for Suicide Prevention. (2012). 2012 National strategy for suicide prevention: Goals and objectives for action, 1–5.

suicide rates than middle-aged and older adults. For instance, in 2016, adolescents and young adults aged 15–24 years had a suicide rate of 13.15.

Suicide rates also vary by race, with the highest rates across all ages occurring among non-Hispanic Native American/Alaska Native and non-Hispanic White populations. Specifically, in 2016, the highest U.S. suicide rate (15.17) was among Whites, and the second highest rate (13.37) was among Native American/Alaska Natives. Much lower and roughly similar rates were found among Asians and Pacific Islanders (6.62) and African Americans (6.03).

Suicide rates similarly differ based on other population characteristics. The following groups have an increased risk of suicide in the general population:

- Men in midlife;
- Older men, especially White men 75 years of age and older;
- Youth, especially American Indian/Alaska Native and LGBT adolescents;
- Individuals with mental health and/or substance use disorders, especially among those with depression, bipolar disorder, and schizophrenia;
- Individuals with serious medical conditions, such as cancer and chronic diseases, that impair functioning and lead to chronic pain;
- Individuals who have previously attempted suicide;
- Individuals who engage in non-suicidal self-injury (NSSI);
- Individuals bereaved by suicide;
- Individuals in criminal justice and child welfare settings.

The most common method of suicide used across all groups in the United States is death by firearm, which accounts for a little more than half (51.4%) of all suicide deaths. The next most common methods include suffocation (including hangings, 24.5%) and poisoning (16.1%). Among the remaining 8%, or approximately 3,275 individuals per year, 781 of those deaths were from jumping. Firearms are the most common method of suicide used by males of all ages, especially those aged 65 years and older. Among females, suffocation is the most common method among those aged 15–24 years, and poisoning is the most common method among women aged 25–64 years.[7]

Regionally, the Mountain West states have some of the highest rates of depression and suicide in the nation. Utah had the highest rate of major depression in 2017, followed by New Mexico. Montana had the

---

Golden Gate Bridge Suicide Demographics

Age

14–24: 14.24%
25–44: 44.85%
45–64: 34.85%
65+: 4.85%
Unknown: 1.21%

Race

African American: 4.24%
Asian: 10.00%
Hispanic: 3.94%
White: 80.30%
Other: 0.91%
Unknown: 0.61%

Sex

Female: 25.76%
Male: 74.24%

Residency

Bay Area: 83.39%
  Alameda: 8.15%
  Contra Costa: 6.58%
  Marin*: 15.67%
  San Mateo: 6.90%
  Napa*: 0.94%
  San Francisco*: 26.33%
  Santa Clara: 9.40%
  Solano: 3.46%
  Sonoma*: 5.96%
Other No. Calif.: 7.52%
So. Calif.: 1.88%
Other U.S.: 6.27%
Out of U.S.: 0.94%

*GG Bridge District Counties: 48.90%

Source: Marin County Coroner's Records 1994–2009

---

highest suicide rate in 2016, followed by Alaska, Wyoming, New Mexico, and Utah. The region has been labeled "the suicide belt."

In a retrospective case history analysis, De Moore and Robertson (1996) identified demographic profiles of 81 people who had engaged in self-harm: those who jumped were more likely to be single, unemployed,

---

7   U.S. Department of Health and Human Services (HHS) Office of the Surgeon General and National Action Alliance for Suicide Prevention. (2012). 2012 National strategy for suicide prevention: Goals and objectives for action, 1–5.

and experiencing psychosis. Those who used firearms were more likely to be male, abuse alcohol, have a forensic history, and have an antisocial or borderline personality disorder.[8] The demographic profile of those who committed suicide by jumping were no more likely to have psychiatric treatment histories than those who didn't and were no more likely to have been psychiatric inpatients in the past. However, 10% of jumpers had a past history of schizophrenia.[9]

Beyond the Numbers

It is important to note that these numbers may not reflect the actual incidences of suicide due to challenges in accurate data collection, compounded by significant delays in the reporting of national and regional rates of suicide attempts and deaths. As such, reported data, across suicide methods, in the United States and worldwide are expected to represent an underestimate of true prevalence. A resource, however, is the web-based Injury Statistics Query and Reporting System (WISQARS®). This interactive, online database provides fatal and nonfatal injury, violent death, and cost of injury data from a variety of trusted sources. With WISQARS, standardized national data on nonfatal injuries, including self-harm, can be compared across demographic groups and by mechanism (in this case, suicidal means). Annual reports are generally available 10–11 months after the end of the calendar year. However, these data carry some limitations. For instance, self-harm data are only available at the national level, and suicide attempts cannot be differentiated from non-suicidal self-harm. Unfortunately, the data are not reliable for tracking trends over the short term, as estimates vary a great deal from year to year. WISQARS' Nonfatal Injury Data webpage can be found at http://www.cdc.gov/injury/wisqars/nonfatal.html.

---

8   De Moore, G., & Robertson, A. (1996). Suicide in the 18 years after deliberate self-harm: A prospective study. *The British Journal of Psychiatry, 169*(4), 489. https://doi.org/10.1192/bjp.169.4.489

9   De Moore, G., & Robertson, A. (1999). Suicide attempts by firearms and by leaping from heights: A comparative study of survivors. *American Journal of Psychiatry, 156*(9), 1425–1431.

Suicide Attempts

As stated previously, for each suicide, estimates suggest there are likely 20 or more suicide attempts. Unlike completed suicides, no total count is kept of suicide attempts in the United States. However, each year, the CDC gathers data from hospitals on nonfatal injuries from self-harm, as well as survey data. According to the American Foundation for Suicide Prevention (AFSP), 505,507 people visited a hospital for injuries due to self-harm in 2015. This number suggests that for every reported suicide death, approximately 11.4 people visit a hospital for self-harm-related injuries. Still, because of the way these data are collected, we are not able to distinguish intentional suicide attempts from non-intentional self-harm behaviors.[10]

Based on the 2016 National Survey of Drug Use and Mental Health, approximately 0.5% of adults aged 18 or older are estimated to have made at least one suicide attempt. This statistic translates to roughly 1.3 million adults. Adult women reported a suicide attempt 1.2 times as often as men.[11]

This trend is also seen in younger age groups. In 2017, 31.5% of students had experienced persistent feelings of sadness or hopelessness in the past year. A significantly higher percentage of female students (41.1%) experienced persistent feelings of sadness or hopelessness than male students (21.4%). A significantly higher percentage of Hispanic students (33.7%) experienced persistent feelings of sadness or hopelessness than White students (30.2%) or Black students (29.2%). There was no significant difference between the percentages of White students and Black students who experienced persistent feelings of sadness or hopelessness.[12]

These types of national, statewide, and regional suicide data are important background information for prevention advocates. However,

---

10   American Foundation for Suicide Prevention. (2020). Suicide statistics. https://afsp.org/suicide-statistics/

11   Substance Abuse and Mental Health Services Administration. (2017). *Key substance use and mental health indicators in the United States: Results from the 2016 National Survey on Drug Use and Health (HHS Publication No. SMA 17-5044, NSDUH Series H-52).* Center for Behavioral Health Statistics and Quality, Substance Abuse and Mental Health Services Administration, 1–86.

12   Division of Adolescent and School Health, National Center for HIV/AIDS, Viral Hepatitis, STD, and TB Prevention. *Youth risk behavior survey: Data sumary & trends report, 2001–2017.* Centers for Disease Control and Prevention, 1–91.

only rarely can these data provide a clear picture for a local suicide hotspot. In most cases, advocates will need to develop custom data from local sources to accurately reflect the danger of problem bridges, rail crossings, or other jump sites. This can be easier said than done, but efforts to collect accurate data at hotspots, cross-referenced with regional and statewide data, are essential to both legitimizing the problem and evaluating the success of the prevention efforts.

Image Credits

Fig. 2.1: Copyright © by John Storey/San Francisco Chronicle.

Organize! Build an Advocacy Program

O ver the years, things had slowly changed at Golden Gate. Thus, as a new suicide prevention advocacy effort began in 2004, three significant social changes would prove to be a foundation for change. An examination of these can help other efforts to organize similar campaigns and suggest how such programs might be successful.

First, there was a shift in transparency. The responsible party—the Golden Gate Bridge, Highway and Transportation District—is a California public agency. Over the years, its behavior has seemed aloof and unresponsive to citizen concerns or the general public interest.[1] Yet, in California, access to the district's meetings and records of its actions were required so the public could understand what was happening. The local and national press also regularly reported on Bridge District actions. Once the Bridge District picked up responsibility for the bus and ferry system, it generated more news and attracted more public interest. Over time—with the press and public now paying more attention—the cozy, introspective self-dealing that had gone on in years past was more difficult to conceal. Thus, the stage was set to hold the district accountable for its actions or inactions.

Second, the Bridge District's governing board became more diverse. The traditional group of politicians and social elite who had served on the board for many years was slowly moved aside to broaden representation. In recent years, labor, ethnic, and LGBT communities—even representatives of the bike-riding public—were added to the district board. And women with leadership experience or political careers have become

---

1   Dyble, L. N. (2009). *Paying the toll: Local power, regional politics, and the Golden Gate Bridge*. Philadelphia: University of Pennsylvania Press, pp. 296.

increasingly represented. Further, San Francisco, with 9 seats on the 19-member Bridge District Board, developed a more diverse appointing authority with the abandonment of countywide election of its 11 member Board of Supervisors in favor of election by geographic district.

Third, despite decades of pleading, persuasion, publicity, and prayer, the district had not been moved to end the suicide problem. However, the district had been moved to action on any number of other issues. In fact, groups as diverse as organized labor and the bicycle coalition had moved the district on their issues of concern. Worker safety and safer bike access—with the installation of a taller fence between the roadway and sidewalk— had all been addressed by Bridge District action. These groups—each with genuine, identifiable constituencies—were organized to be assertive, coordinated, insistent, and, unlike the previous efforts for a suicide barrier, capable of conducting advocacy over an extended period. In reviewing past efforts at stopping suicide at the bridge, most of the groups had, indeed, been organized, but the organizational characteristics associated with successful groups advocating for bridge workers or bike riders were not present in suicide prevention efforts. Quite simply, earlier suicide prevention efforts could not sustain a campaign. The previous efforts had raised concern but gone silent or inactive once district opposition proved to be stronger than anticipated. However, the success of other advocates had proven that—with a properly focused campaign—the Bridge District could be pushed to change.

In addition, advocates saw that opposition to suicide prevention efforts was "soft." There were no sharply focused economic interests

FIGURE 3.1 The Golden Gate Bridge installed the barrier on the right—between the walkway and traffic—quickly and with little controversy. At the time of this installation, there had been over 1,200 suicide jumps from the short railing on the left.

challenged by the effort. Opposition would be largely based on popular but faulty arguments about the nature of suicide, concerns about bridge aesthetics, and securing approval and funding for the suicide prevention structure itself.

Old assumptions about suicide could be challenged when the facts were properly marshaled, presented clearly, and repeated at every opportunity. Restricting access to lethal means was an established suicide prevention measure, but few in the public or at the Bridge District understood this. Likewise, the fact that, given time, a suicidal impulse can pass and the urge toward self-destruction fade were not concepts well understood in the culture.

The aesthetic concerns were quite real, but also could be managed. The bridge is a beloved national landmark with significant historic importance. A thoughtful campaign, with well-conceived visuals, and ultimately a well-designed solution would be required. Early on, a quality presentation of what a suicide prevention structure might look like was of immense importance. Without a good representation of a proposed suicide prevention structure, an often cynical public might assume the worst and rally in opposition. It was also likely that the district's history—having once proposed barbwire and later cattle fencing to help prevent

FIGURE 3.2 The short rail along the pedestrian walkway on the Golden Gate Bridge is easy to climb.

suicides—would feed those fears. Therefore, any suicide prevention structure required great sensitivity to the aesthetics of the installation.

As daunting as these challenges might be, there were no major financial concerns likely to be in opposition. The effort would threaten no entrenched capital interests, and speculative interests, such as real estate or technology sectors, were untouched by the issue. The bridge is a major tourist attraction, and the public airing of its suicide reputation did, naturally, cause some concern within the tourism industry. This concern, however, worked in favor of bringing an end to the suicide problem.

The Spark

The 21st-century effort to end suicide on the Golden Gate Bridge began with the work of a single journalist. Tad Friend published a long exposé of the bridge's suicide problem in the *New Yorker* issue of October 13, 2003. Friend spoke with survivors of suicide jumps, families who suffered suicide loss, Bridge District leaders, and prevention advocates to ascertain why the problem persisted. Although the *New Yorker* is well read in California and the Bridge District was certainly aware of the publication, there was no visible public reaction to the article. The PFNC did begin to organize a task force to attack the problem, and while the task force began work, word came out that a documentary film crew was out to capture the story as well.

A Fire Breaks Out

News of Eric Steel's documentary *The Bridge* became public in 2005—a year before its release. District voices, from the staff and board, were outraged, angry, and wildly wrong in their description of the film.[2] Steel had not told the Golden Gate Bridge leadership that he was there to document the suicide problem, and they cried foul. With the death count at the Bridge then over 1,300, the word from the district was that by exposing the story, a grave injustice had been done to the bridge itself.

2   Bateson, J. (2012). *The Final Leap: Suicide on the Golden Gate Bridge*. Berkeley: University of California Press.

Nevertheless, the district felt compelled to call a hearing on the matter. Just before that hearing, Jonathan Zablotny, a popular San Francisco high school senior, jumped to his death. His classmates wanted to tackle the problem and came together to confront the Bridge District Board. They were joined by many others also crushed by a suicide within their network of family or friends. Copied below is the *San Francisco Chronicle* description of the hearing:

> The board, seated around a vast, oblong table, listened all morning to individual stories of suicide. So many people showed up with photos of their loved ones that some had to wait in the hallway. One by one, they stood or sat at the end of the table and spoke, a funeral procession of mothers and fathers, sisters and brothers, boyfriends and girlfriends, teachers and classmates. Knowing the statistics—18–20 suicides a year from the bridge, around 1,300 since it opened—still doesn't prepare you for the weight of the grief in a room packed with people who have endured such pain and loss. You wonder how a person hearing these stories could ever view the bridge the same way again.

> Joan Ryan
> *San Francisco Chronicle*
> March 12, 2005

At the conclusion of the hearing, the Bridge District called for a set of studies to review preliminary designs for a suicide deterrent system, testing of these designs under the wind conditions common at the Gate, and completion of the required environmental assessment. Because the Golden Gate Bridge is a dynamic suspension bridge that can move up and down and east and west as the winds blow, the load on the bridge changes, or the earth underneath moves in an earthquake, ensuring the bridge would not fail as a result of any structural additions is a particular concern. A similar suspension bridge in Tacoma, Washington, had collapsed in 40-mph winds in 1940. Likewise, the design of a suicide barrier was of great public interest, and several options had to be considered. One caveat was attached to the proposed study: the district would allocate no funds to the effort.

As a result of public controversy generated by Steel's film and the early organizing by the PFNC and its task force, as 2005 progressed, momentum picked up for resolving the suicide problem. Among the developments were the following:

- A group of UC–Berkeley engineering students produced a set of scale-model suicide barriers, complete with preliminary engineering calculations. The models provided an early visual sense of what a suicide barrier might look like and were well received. Through the magic of Photoshop®, the students' models were added to a photograph of the bridge. This provided advocates with a photo-realistic representation of several barrier options. These in turn were used to demonstrate that attractive suicide prevention structures were feasible. Their work received extensive press coverage and was later published in the influential *Journal of Architectural Engineering*. (*Journal of Architectural Engineering*, Vol. 13, Issue 1, March 2007)

- The *San Francisco Chronicle* ran a five-part, front-page feature on the bridge suicide problem. Many of the interviews were with family members who had lost relatives to bridge suicides.

FIGURE 3.3 The bridge as it is and with the photo-realistic addition of three suicide barriers proposed by UC–Berkeley engineering students Danielle Hutchings, Ryan Stauffer, Douglas Wahl, and Robert Simpson. Photoshop revisions by Nick Fain.

- Marin County coroner Ken Holmes began releasing an annual report on the bridge suicide toll. His report included deaths recorded in other counties and persons missing but presumed dead from a bridge jump. Demographic data were also made public.

- Kevin Hines launched a national speaking program. He had survived a suicide attempt from the bridge and, following a long recovery, was featured in Eric Steel's film. He would now carry his story forward personally to audiences throughout the United States.

In addition, families who had lost loved ones to a bridge suicide began to organize and push for a barrier. Many of them had spoken with great pain at the district's hearing, and they wanted the problem resolved. The deep anger many harbored toward the district, which had done so little to stop suicide for decades, became stronger and more vocal.

The PFNC's informational meetings with these families did not seem adequate for those who wanted a more active role in the fight. Eventually, Dave Hull, whose daughter Kathy had died at the bridge, and Patrick Hines, the father of jump survivor Kevin Hines, began looking for a different approach. Meanwhile, within the PFNC task force, Paul Muller began pushing for a closer working relationship with the Bay Area Suicide and Crisis Intervention Alliance (BASCIA)—a coalition of suicide prevention agencies in the region. Once PFNC decided to maintain its existing approach—with a limited role for surviving family members—and Muller was told to leave, Hull and Hines asked him to join their fledgling effort. They began meeting with the Althea Foundation to discuss an expanded advocacy project. Althea founder Alexsis de Raandt St. James agreed the bridge suicide problem needed to be addressed in a more comprehensive manner and funded the launch of the Bridge Rail Foundation. This new not-for-profit foundation would take a more aggressive and strategically focused effort to stop suicide at the Golden Gate Bridge. Two additional members joined Hull, Hines, and Muller at Bridge Rail's initial meetings—Renee Amochaev, who had lost a good friend to Golden Gate Bridge suicide, and Marin County coroner Ken Holmes.

The Bridge Rail Foundation was born with a clear, singular focus—stop the suicides on the Golden Gate. It would maintain that singular goal until the construction contract was signed in January 2017. This strategic focus would sustain Bridge Rail through a campaign that lasted more than a decade. In addition, this focus would attract new supporters whose families had recently suffered a suicide loss as a result of a bridge jump. These new advocates would bring time, energy, and persistence to the effort that was unique. The stories of their personal experiences with a preventable tragedy was powerful testimony that could not be ignored. And in telling their stories and sharing them with the public, they were fighting to prevent the tragedy they experienced from continuing to engulf even more families. Bridge Rail provided an organization through which they could engage the fight.

Implicit in the definitions of both community organizing and community building is the concept of empowerment, viewed as an enabling process through which individuals or communities take control over their lives and environments. A multilevel construct, empowerment involves participation, control, and critical awareness.[3]

Any casual look at the history of community organizing will often reveal serious splits that develop among organizations that appear to have the same goals. Commonly, these organizations become frozen in a competitive stew, unable to act except in competition or in counter-position to each other. That scenario did not happen between Bridge Rail and PFNC. Each continued to push the issue, advocate as they saw best, and stay with the fight as long as they could. As it turned out, Bridge Rail gathered most of the support and energy to push forward, whereas PFNC lost steam and eventually joined with Bridge Rail as the prime advocacy organization. But the stable and continuous dedication to the primary goal remained with each organization, and each stayed true to the constituent base they developed. For PFNC, its base included psychiatrists and the professional medical community, whereas surviving family members, their supporters, and local suicide prevention advocates worked more closely with the Bridge Rail Foundation.

---

3   Zimmerman, M., & Rappaport, J. (1988). Citizen participation, perceived control, and psychological empowerment. *American Journal of Community Psychology, 16*(5), 725–750. https://doi.org/10.1007/BF00930023

Leadership style or practice is important to consider at this point. Bridge Rail adopted a focused insistence on stopping suicides at the Golden Gate Bridge and actively worked to steer supporters in a positive and effective direction, but it did not insist on one "correct" path. Rather, the foundation listened to counter-views, adopted some, quietly supported others, and actively opposed only the most extreme or counterproductive approaches as the advocacy program proceeded.

Many supporters wanted to simply beat up the Bridge District, seen as the perpetrators responsible for allowing the death of a loved one to occur. Still others had deep personal revulsion at the district's constant attempts to look "reasonable" when a profound—and preventable—tragedy had befallen their families and hundreds of others. For example, over the years, the district had proposed many barrier designs. Yet, no project was accepted, designs were never fully fleshed out, and funding was never established. Additionally, after the crisis phones were installed in the 1990s, the district never evaluated the effectiveness of this system, nor did they report the status of the suicide problem to the public. Thus, there was little faith in the district's "reasonableness." Bridge Rail's approach was to never minimize the tragedy and never allow the district off the hook. The district was the responsible party, and it was responsible for fixing the problem. The only question was, would it?

Within a year of that first hearing, San Francisco supervisor and bridge director Tom Ammiano persuaded the MTC to release funds for the preliminary environmental studies. Ammiano was the first San Francisco public official to actively engage the campaign in the 21st century, and he would stick with the fight for over a decade while serving as county supervisor in San Francisco and later as a state assembly member. He would also provide the key link between advocates and other elected officials in the state capital, Sacramento, and Washington, D.C.

Work on these studies got underway in 2006. Results from the wind tunnel tests were released in the summer of 2007, confirming what engineers had been saying since the 1950s—a properly designed railing or net system would not adversely affect the bridge. A set of preliminary designs was released in the summer of 2008. Included were five alternatives—most similar to work done in the 1970s and 1990s and by the UC–Berkeley engineering students. The one new element was a safety net set 20 feet below the deck surface and extending 20 feet out from the bridge. Research by the district's architects into suicide prevention safety structures had uncovered a net system in Bern, Switzerland, that had proved quite successful. This system not only stopped the suicides; it stopped the jumping altogether.

FIGURE 3.4 The suicide deterrent net as proposed by the Golden Gate Bridge District in a photo-realistic image. This representation was widely circulated and often reproduced in the press as the debate on its construction progressed. It provided advocates with an unmistakable presentation of just what was proposed at the bridge and calmed many concerns about the visual impact of the effort to reduce suicides. The net design is based on a system installed in Bern, Switzerland, which reduced suicides to zero in its first 10 years of existence. A key to the design is the 20-ft. drop from the bridge deck to the net, creating a nonfatal jump while the resultant injuries limit the jumper's ability to pursue a further fall.

While these studies progressed, Bridge Rail maintained an active campaign. A key to the organizing was to open avenues of participation for many of those concerned. Thus, Bridge Rail found increasing opportunities for volunteers. These included:

- Speaking on the need for a suicide barrier;

- Researching the nature of bridge suicides and suicide prevention;

- Organizing events to promote the construction of a suicide barrier;

- Joining events organized by suicide prevention agencies;

- Staffing informational booths at the fund-raising walks organized by the American Foundation for Suicide Prevention (AFSP).

Whereas these activities are discussed in greater detail in later chapters, they all directly contributed to the goal of stopping suicides on the Golden Gate Bridge. They also made the organization stronger and more flexible, providing volunteers who had differing skills and interests with opportunities to actively participate. As a result, when major decisions were considered at the Bridge District, the MTC, or other public agencies, Bridge Rail had an active core of volunteers to call on for testimony or direct support.

As the suicide deaths continued at the bridge, surviving family members would often contact the foundation, asking what they might do to push the issue forward. In many cases, Bridge Rail president Dave Hull would simply encourage survivors—with no formal training—to tell their stories at the Bridge District board meetings during the public comment segment of their regular agenda. Over time, Bridge Rail's core of volunteers continued to grow, which ensured that it had the staying power to stick with the issue. The preventable suicides at the Golden Gate would not fade from the consciousness of the Bridge District or general public, as it had so many times before.

Bridge Rail also organized major events that drew in the public and generated press interest throughout the campaign. One unique approach—the *Whose Shoes?* exhibit—became a particularly powerful dramatization of the magnitude of death at the Golden Gate Bridge. First launched just southeast of the Golden Gate on Crissy Field during an AFSP-sponsored walk, the exhibit displayed over 1,300 pairs of shoes, representing every one of the suicides from the bridge to date. Featured at the center of the exhibit was a pair of WWI U.S. Army boots, symbolically standing in for Harold Wobber, a war veteran who was the first known suicide from the bridge. The display also created a productive opportunity for volunteers to get the word out and supplied a powerful visual that generated press attention. Collecting the shoes for the exhibit proved a unique opportunity, as well. Several families donated shoes from loved ones lost to bridge suicide, and other donations were received from concerned individuals, as well as business and local labor organizations. A sporting goods retailer proved to be the largest donor. Whereas the first *Whose Shoes?* exhibits proved successful, a more sophisticated display and better venue would take the power of the display far forward in the coming years.

Meanwhile, formal planning and evaluation activities proceeded within the Bridge District. In October 2008, after extensive public hearings and still more press coverage, the district finally accepted the idea that some physical deterrent system was necessary. The board voted for

FIGURE 3.5 At the center of every Bridge Rail Foundation *Whose Shoes?* exhibit was a pair of WWI U.S. Army boots. They stand for Harold Wobber, the war veteran who was the first known suicide from the Golden Gate Bridge.

the suicide deterrent net proposal and designated it as the preferred option. The staff was instructed to complete the environmental assessment on that design. That review was completed and finally approved by the Bridge District Board on February 12, 2010. In July 2010, the MTC designated funds that allowed the Bridge District to complete the design and engineering drawings for the proposed net. This critical phase of the project was now finally funded.

Whereas the organizing efforts by Bridge Rail focused on families and suicide prevention agencies, there were others who made important contributions as the issue progressed toward resolution. Most obvious was the success seen with the student engineers' design project at UC–Berkeley. The foundation approached the engineering department a second time, and a new group of students produced additional engineering and construction calculations. The foundation also saw contributions from both faculty and students at other institutions as well. When the value of suicide prevention on bridges was questioned by faculty from a Southern California school, UC–San Francisco faculty presented to the Bridge District Board a complete discussion of the issue, pointing to the errors in the original paper and describing the weight of repeated peer-reviewed studies that supported access restriction as a suicide prevention measure on bridges. The University of San Francisco Department of Politics hosted a major conference and organizing event that Bridge Rail created to bring advocates together for a planning session. Stanford faculty joined the Bridge Rail board. Outside the Bay Area, journalism students from North Carolina and Western Kentucky Universities produced documentaries on suicide survivor families that won first and second place in the national Hearst Journalism Awards Program multimedia category. But the UC–Berkeley contributions were distinct and numerous. Students and graduate students in history, public policy, journalism, public health, and engineering all contributed to the long, drawn-out effort.

Others provided key constituents to the effort. Certainly, the psychiatrists organized by PFNC maintained a constant regular presence in the fight. PFNC president Mel Blaustein, MD, testified at every major hearing on the issue and regularly spoke before medical groups throughout the area. So, too, did local suicide prevention organizations. No hearing took place without Eve Meyer of SF Suicide Prevention and her close allies in Marin, Alameda, Contra Costa, Santa Clara, San Mateo, and, occasionally, Los Angeles counties testifying as to the need. Likewise, the AFSP, whose local chapter included a family member with a son lost to a bridge suicide, provided the fight with ongoing support. This support included speaking opportunities at their fund-raising events and direct support as needed in Washington, D.C., and the state capital of Sacramento.

The strategy used by Bridge Rail to simply focus on a call to stop the suicides at the Golden Gate Bridge and organize supporters to take that message forward at every opportunity ensured eventual success. As an all-volunteer organization, Bridge Rail was able to coordinate a program that would maintain a constant presence before the Bridge District. This work included:

- Advocating for funding through regional transportation agencies;
- Encouraging political support;
- Maintaining an active press relations program;
- Sponsoring events for the general public; and
- Communicating through digital media.

Each of these activities fed off each other, strengthening the effort and ensuring it could prevail over the extended time the advocacy required. Key elements of this process are discussed in subsequent chapters, but the basic framework Bridge Rail developed sustained volunteers to be assertive, coordinated, and insistent. In short, the effort was organized and found success through regular communications and a persistent approach to advocacy.

Image Credits

Communicate!

Going Public

Any public advocacy campaign requires a thoughtful communications strategy. To do so, you must first gather the facts, identify your audience or audiences, and make use of the communication means available to you. As the push for a suicide barrier on the Golden Gate Bridge progressed, that is exactly how Bridge Rail advocates approached the communications challenge.

The first communications challenge was to simply gather the facts.

Capturing the Complete Picture

Tad Friend's article in the *New Yorker* appeared as the suicide toll surpassed 1,200 in late 2003, but that number was not well known. In fact, most people were so uninformed that during the Bridge District's 2005 hearing, a district director asked the staff if there had been any additional deaths since "that poor girl from Santa Rosa" had jumped in December of 2001. The staff and attending public, which included Renee Milligan, the *poor girl*'s mother, gasped at the ignorance of the question. District records would indicate there had been at least 80 confirmed or suspected suicides since the death of Marissa Imrie, Milligan's daughter. That advocates would have to present a clear understanding of the facts about death at the Golden Gate Bridge was apparent, starting with the actual body count.

However, the body count alone was not sufficient. Telling the world just who those people were in life was also necessary. This task involved much more than merely completing the story. Confronting several popular myths about suicide in general and at the bridge in particular was also involved. Among these myths was a belief that people came from all over—from other states, Canada, Mexico, Europe, and Asia—to jump from the Golden Gate. The assumption was that there was no way to stop them and therefore little reason to try. In addition, there was a generalized sense that the jumpers had not been productive citizens. Occasionally, this idea was expressed as hostility toward those with mental illness, but other times it was simply couched as sympathetic-sounding inaction. One would hear an expression like, "It's too bad about them, but what can be done?" This myth dovetailed well with the idea that suicide itself was not preventable and that once the decision to take your life was made, it was irreversible. Addressing these attitudes would be impossible if advocates were not able to describe who had died at the bridge and what the community was losing in their deaths. Likewise, the firsthand experiences of those who attempted suicide and survived would be of critical importance. Therefore, advocates would need three things:

- a solid statistical representation of suicide at the bridge;

- a presentation of published research on suicidal behavior; and

- personal stories of people with direct experience of attempts and loss.

A unique set of circumstances at Golden Gate would work to Bridge Rail's benefit in securing and presenting the data on deaths. When a jump is suspected, district security staff or the California Highway Patrol calls the U.S. Coast Guard for a rescue attempt. Because a jump from the bridge is a 225-foot fall into very cold water, survival is rare. Most die from the blunt force trauma of the impact, and those who survive the impact are badly injured and usually drown. Thus, the Coast Guard's rescue work is more often a recovery-of-remains effort. When a body is found, it's taken to the Coast Guard station in Marin County—the community just north of San Francisco—and turned over to the county coroner's office. At the time, Marin's coroner, Ken Holmes, was an elected official with a great deal of independence in how the office was run. He was also active in Marin's suicide prevention efforts. When approached about data gathering for the bridge project, Holmes welcomed the effort and provided access to the public files.

The coroner's data revealed much more than the body count. Holmes's investigators had recorded all the basic demographics—age, race, gender, occupation, hometown, and related data. This information was first compiled and released by the PFNC. As the advocacy effort moved forward, Holmes joined the newly formed Bridge Rail Foundation and began to issue yearly reports on Golden Gate suicide deaths. However, his office was merged with the county sheriff's office in 2011, and Bridge Rail's access to suicide data was reduced. Still, a detailed picture of what was happening had been established with 15 years of detailed information on the deaths. The communications program could now describe who was dying at the bridge in much more detail than had ever been presented before. A summary of the last report is included in the sidebar in Chapter 2 and a listing of occupations is in the sidebar here.

Last Known Occupation

Listed below—in alphabetical order—is the last known occupation of those who died by a bridge suicide from 1994 to 2009.

Accountant • Accountant • Accountant • Accountant • Accountant Clerk • Administrative Assistant • Administrative Assistant • Administrator • Advertising Art Director • Aide to Retarded • Architect • Art Dealer • Artist • Artist • Artist • Artist • Artist • Artist • Attorney • Attorney • Auto Painter • Bank Teller • Bartender • Bartender • Bell Man • Billiard Player • Book Sales Person • Broadcast Production Assistant • Bus Driver • Business Manager • Business Owner • Business Owner • Card Dealer • Caregiver • Carpenter • Carpenter • Carpenter • Cartographer • Cashier • Cashier • Chef • Chef • Child Psychologist • Chiropractor • Cleaning • Clerk • Clerk • Computer Engineer • Computer Engineer • Computer Game Designer • Computer Operator • Computer Programmer • Computer Programmer • Computer Programmer • Computer Scientist • Computer Technician • Computer Technician • Construction • Construction Laborer • Construction Worker • Consultant Psychologist • Cook • Cook • Counselor • Counselor • Custodial • Custodian • Dentist • Disabled • Disabled • Disabled • Disabled • Driver • Driver • Educator • Electrical Engineer • Electrical Engineer • Electrical Engineer • Electrical Engineer • Electrical Engineer • Electrician • Engineer • Environmental Specialist • Factory Worker • Fashion Designer • Film Animator • Financial • Financial • Firefighter • Florist • Food Business Partner • Food Delivery • Food Service • Food Service • Food Service • Forklift Operator • Foster Care Recruiter • Frame Maker • Funeral Director • Gardner • General Contractor • General Contractor • Glazier • Grant Administrator • Grocery Bagger • Handyman • Health Services Supervisor • High School Student • Homemaker • Homemaker • Homemaker • Homemaker • Homemaker

• Homemaker • Homemaker • Homemaker • Homemaker • Hotel Valet • Housekeeper • Internet Designer • Investment Owner • Investor • Investor • Investor • Journalist • Laborer • Laborer • Laborer • Laborer • Landscaper • Landscaper • Lawyer • Lawyer • Librarian • Loan Officer • Machinist • Mail Worker • Maintenance Worker • Marketing • Mechanic • Mechanic • Mechanic • Mechanic • Mechanic • Mental Health Support Worker • Merchant Marine • Metal Recycler • Metal Worker • Military • Military • Military • Molecular Biologist • Mortgage Broker • Mortgage Broker • Music Production • Musician • Musician • Network Administrator • Never Worked • Never Worked • Never Worked • Never Worked • Never Worked • Never Worked • None • None • Nurse Caregiver • Nursing Assistant • Office Clerk • Office Technician • Office Worker • Optometrist • Optometrist • Painter • Painting Contractor • Painting Contractor • Paralegal • Park Supervisor • Personal Services • Philosopher • Photographer • Physical Therapist • Physician • Plumber • Poet • Police Clerk • Political Consultant • Postal Clerk • Printer • Printer • Probation Officer • Programmer • Proofreader • Proprietor • Psychiatrist • Psychologist • Psychologist • Psychologist • Psychotherapist • Public Relations • Radiation Monitor • Radio Show Talk Host • Real Estate Agent • Realtor • Realtor • Receptionist • Restaurant Manager • Retail Clerk • Retail Clerk • Retail Manager • Retail Manager • Retail Manager • Sales • Sales • Sales • Sales • Sales • Sales • Sales & Marketing • Sales Clerk • Sales Person • Sales Rep • Sales Rep • Salesman • Salesman • Salesman • Salesman • Secretary • Secretary • Secretary • Security Guard • Security Guard • Security Guard • Security Guard • Security Officer • Security Guard • Senior Editor • Singer • Social Worker • Social Worker • Social Worker • Social Worker • Software Consultant • Software Engineer • Software Engineer • Software Engineer • Software Engineer • Stationary Engineer • Stockman • Store Owner • Store Wrapper • Student • Taxi Driver • Teacher • Teacher • Teacher • Teacher • Teacher • Teacher • Teacher • Teacher • Teacher • Technician • Telemarketer • Telemarketer • Teller • Translator • Tree Trimmer • Tutor • Tutor • Unemployed • Various • Vocational Ed Specialist • Waiter • Waiter • Waiter • Web Designer • Web Designer • Welder • Welder • Writer • Writer • Writer

Source: The Bridge Rail Foundation, "A Fifteen-Year Report: Golden Gate Bridge Suicide Demographics," p. 5.

Holmes's records made clear the deaths were a Bay Area problem, for more than 80% of those who died in Golden Gate Bridge suicides were Bay Area residents. Likewise, most of those who died had been employed, productive members of society. The occupation list of more than 300 individuals shows blue-collar, white-collar, executive, and professional employment; In previous years, even members of the clergy had taken their lives at the Golden Gate. Still, some were never employed, but they represented a small sector of jumpers. Bridge Rail took this information and made it pubic. The information was posted to Bridge Rail's website, and when new data were available, Bridge Rail organized press events. These events included a yearly January release of the annual death toll from the coroner's office and a special 15-year data presentation released on September 9, 2009.

Present the Research

However, demographic data were only part of the story. Medical research-ers added a great deal to our understanding of suicidal behavior since the mid-1970s. This information showed that prevention was possible and would save lives. Like many discoveries in science, the first major finding of an important suicide prevention strategy was discovered by accident. Remember the phrase "go stick your head in the oven"? It comes from Great Britain, when coal gas was used as household cooking gas. Coal gas has a high concentration of poisonous carbon monoxide. As a result, inhaling cooking gas—with your head in an unlit oven—was a popular means of suicide until Britain changed to natural gas, with a low carbon monoxide concentration. The result was a 26% drop in the suicide rate in the study area. Additional research shows the drop was attributable to a decrease in carbon monoxide deaths with no significant increase of suicide by other means.[1]

The coal gas situation sparked a much deeper investigation into suicidal behavior and prevention. Researchers addressed questions, such as why suicidal people did not simply use other available lethal means, why there was a distinct gender difference in means of suicide, and what would happen if other means of suicide were also restricted.

---

[1]   Kreitman, N. (1976). The coal gas story. United Kingdom suicide rates, 1960–71. *British Journal of Preventive & Social Medicine, 30*(2), 86–93. https://doi. org/10.1136/jech.30.2.86

Over the next several decades, findings emerged showing that suicides could be reduced if access to guns, pills, and poisons was restricted. And research specific to bridges and other jump sites also emerged. Finding after finding reinforced a simple concept in suicide prevention: if access to lethal means was restricted, suicides would decrease.

Bridge Rail advocates assembled a summary of the research findings on suicide prevention and access restriction. This summary was then reported in public testimony and referred to online and in print. Three major points emerged among the findings:

1. Research on suicide has consistently shown that if access to a single means of suicide is restricted, overall suicides decrease.

   In a comprehensive review of all the scientific literature on suicide, 23 physicians and scientists from the United States, Europe, and Asia concluded that restricting access to lethal means is one of only two scientifically established methods to reduce suicides.[2]

   More suicides in the United States are from gunshots than any other means. Seventeen published studies showed the rate of suicide death in gun-owning households was at least three times greater than in households where guns were not present. But where guns were present, proper safety procedures—gun locks and securing the ammo—cut the risk of suicide by two thirds.[3]

   Use of prescription and over-the-counter drugs has been a means of suicide for many years. However, the availability of these drugs changed, and as it changed, the number of suicides changed as well. For instance, in Australia, suicide from sedative overdose increased when the drugs became easier to get and decreased when access was restricted. In the United Kingdom, limiting access to an over-the-counter drug—by simply changing the packaging requirements—reduced the number of suicides.[4]

---

2   Mann, J. J., Apter, A., Bertolote, J., et al. (2005). Suicide prevetion strategies: A systematic review. *Journal of the American Medical Association, 294*(16): 2064–2074.

3   Simon, R. (2007). Gun safety management with patients at risk for suicide. *Suicide and Life-Threatening Behavior, 37*(5), 518–526. https://doi.org/10.1521/suli.2007.37.5.518

4   Gunnell, D., & Frankel, S. (1994). Prevention of suicide: Aspirations and evidence. *BMJ: British Medical Journal, 308*(6938), 1227–1233. https://doi.org/10.1136/bmj.308.6938.1227

2. A suicidal state is a temporary condition—lives can be saved when a suicidal person gets past the immediate urge to die.

One study in Texas looked at 153 cases of near-lethal suicide attempts. Researchers found that 24% of these individuals had spent less than 5 minutes between the decision to commit suicide and the attempt.[5]

Another study of suicides in the Montréal subway found that 100 of the 129 individuals studied had an adverse life event within 2 weeks of the death.[6]

Cognitive tests for impaired decision making consistently showed higher scores for suicidal individuals than controls in national studies.[7]

3. Bridge Rail had direct evidence that lives could be saved at the Golden Gate Bridge.

Dr. Richard Seiden of UC–Berkeley's School of Public Health investigated the lives of more than 500 people removed from the Golden Gate Bridge when they were about to jump. He found that 94% of these people were either still alive or had died of natural causes after 26 years, on average, following the suicide attempt.[8] Of the first 26 people known to have survived a jump from the Golden Gate Bridge, only one was known to have subsequently died by suicide.[9]

The research and demographic information the advocates assembled was the most complete information ever made available in the push to stop

5   Simon, T., Swann, A., Powell, K., & Potter, L. (2001). Characteristics of impulsive suicide attempts and attempters. *Suicide & Life-Threatening Behavior, 32,* 49–59. Retrieved from http://search.proquest.com/docview/224873474/

6   Mishara, B. (1999). Suicide in the Montreal Subway System: Characteristics of the victims, antecedents and implications for prevention. *Can J Psychiatry, 44*(7): 690–696.

7   Jollant, F. (2015). Neurocognitive impairments in suicide attempters and their relatives. *European Psychiatry, 30.*

8   Seiden, R. (1978). Where are they now? A follow-up study of suicide attempters from the Golden Gate Bridge. *Suicide and Life-Threatening Behavior, 8*(4), 203–216.

9   Rosen, David. (1975). Suicide survivors. A follow-up study of persons who survived jumping from the Golden Gate and San Francisco Oakland Bay Bridges. *The Western Journal of Medicine,* 122, 289–294.

the suicides at the Golden Gate Bridge. In truth, however, bits and pieces of this information had been presented to the district before—some as far back as the 1970s. Over the decades, those leading the charge on suicide prevention at the Golden Gate Bridge varied, from the medical community to the faith community to established suicide prevention agencies, and all had brought the prevention message to the district. After the publication of Friend's *New Yorker* article, many of these same people were motivated to try again. Yet, past records showed these efforts had simply not been convincing. To be sure, all these groups were genuinely concerned and very much wanted to see the suicides at the Golden Gate Bridge end, but it became clear that a stronger and more powerful voice was needed.

The Most Powerful Voices

Just who might be the most powerful advocates came from the first press conference organized by the PFNC. Renee Milligan had spoken about her lost daughter. She would be the first among the hundreds of families and friends who had lost loved ones to a bridge suicide to speak out. Surviving family members and friends would prove to be the core of the movement to stop these suicides. Their stories, their pain, and the power of their persistence and presentation were not to be denied. They presented to the public a new voice, one not heard from in the past, and their personal experiences with suicide at the Golden Gate ensured they had the fortitude to never go away, never fold up the tent and accept that things could not be done. They became a clear and distinct force and found that, in losing a family member, they could give life to the movement for change. They would see that the pain they suffered would no longer be the experience of other families in the Bay Area once suicide was prevented at the bridge.

Most importantly, these advocates were communicating. They were an articulate and aggressive cadre of people ready to tell their stories to anyone who would listen. To these unique voices, the press listened. Their personal stories were circulated through print, radio interviews, TV news programs, and other interview settings. The national media was interested as well in the story of a popular landmark with a serious suicide problem, and the issue received major in-depth coverage in the *Los Angeles Times*, the *Washington Post*, and the *New York Times*.

These new advocates gave powerful testimonies before the Bridge District with the hope that others would not suffer the same way. As the deaths continued to mount and critical decisions were held up by the Bridge District board and other public agencies, families with recent suicides would appear to tell their stories. One such family attended a district hearing, spoke, then rushed out of the meeting. They had an appointment with a funeral director to plan the memorial for their recently lost daughter.

A communications strategy evolved that was anchored around the belief that the bridge suicide problem had to be addressed publicly and kept fresh in the public's mind. The program was geared toward several key audiences, stayed consistent in its message, and remained sensitive to the need to tailor its message for each audience and repeat it at every opportunity. Throughout the campaign, advocates always focused on what action needed to be taken—stop the suicides on the Golden Gate Bridge.

The first step, then, was quite simple—have the family members and friends tell their stories directly to the Bridge District. Many survivor families took this opportunity—some for one meeting, others at times when the district would schedule a key decision. In the last few years of the fight, the Gamboa family—father Manuel, mother Kymberlyrenee, or both—began attending every district board meeting, speaking at every one. The people who made the decisions would never be allowed to escape the story.

Bridge Rail advocates knew, however, that simply pushing the district for action was not sufficient. Engaging other decision makers and the general public was also necessary. The campaign needed to develop opportunities to get the story of what was happening at the bridge out. Likewise, ensuring that other suicide prevention advocates and agencies and the mental health community were fully informed of the project and ways in which they could join in the effort was also necessary. Additionally, particular attention was addressed to key decision makers in transportation funding. Finally, the significance of suicide prevention in general and restricting easy access to other lethal bridges and jump sites was important to include as well.

Along the way, Bridge Rail adopted several principles that guided its efforts and ensured that a credible presence before the media was maintained. With any advocacy program, there is a temptation to exaggerate the degree of the problem to be addressed. It's a natural tendency but one that can often work to undermine credibility and turn off interested reporters and the media. Bridge Rail knew that—thanks to the unique cooperation of the Marin coroner's office—the facts were enough and that the bare truth was sufficiently horrible to demand action. Thus, simply publishing and providing the media with the clear undisputed facts was a reliable basis for long-term success.

Bridge Rail made use of the annual reports by Marin coroner Ken Holmes, and the yearly toll became a regular January press release. Some reporters even came to expect and occasionally requested the report before the data were prepared.

Suicides at the Golden Gate also generated occasional feature stories through the initiative of individual reporters. In these cases, Bridge Rail provided insights and arranged for persons willing to be interviewed for print and on-camera news coverage. Bridge Rail board members Dave Hull and Dayna Whitmer were frequently quoted, as were John Brooks, Kymberlyrenee and Manuel Gamboa, and others. Expert comments were also arranged with Ken Holmes and SF Suicide Prevention head Eve Meyer. In addition to helping arrange many of these interviews, Bridge Rail continued to make data and background information available to the press to fill out their stories or provide context for the news. Meanwhile, suicide jump survivor Kevin Hines continued to develop his national speaking program that both riveted audiences and generated press coverage as he traveled around the country.

FIGURE 4.1 Bridge Rail Foundation made members readily available for interview by the media. Here BRF president Dave Hull is interviewed.

Among the Bay Area press, local newspapers, including the *San Francisco Chronicle* and the *Marin Independent Journal,* were most interested. And whereas the Marin paper has a relatively small circulation, its owners manage a newsgroup, which ensures that any story the *Independent Journal* publishes also appears in publications serving Santa Clara, Alameda, and Contra Costa counties, whose populations cover about 75% of the San Francisco Bay Area. These two papers provided wide coverage for the entire Bay Area. Local television stations were also interested, with Oakland's KTVU and San Francisco's KGO initiating stories and coverage of press events the Bridge Rail organized.

Digital Media

The most recent push for a suicide barrier on the bridge parallels the development and growth of digital media in the 21st century. From the start, advocates understood the importance of a strong web presence, and the Bridge Rail Foundation made extensive use of technology early on to create an informative website. In addition, as social media developed, many supporters were making good use of the services. BRF board member Dayna Whitmer launched a Facebook® page for the foundation and maintained a regular presence, posting as the decision-making process progressed on the Golden Gate suicide deterrent net project. In addition, the Bridge Rail newsletter was made a regular feature through the efforts of board member John Bateson. These services, with the later addition of Twitter®, served to maintain and strengthen the foundation's ties with its most active members, expedite communications when important events, hearings, or decisions by the district or other agencies were pending, and enhance connections with the broader suicide prevention community. Bridge Rail's online presence is strengthened with links and networking to other related sites concerned about Golden Gate suicides, such as Bridgewatch Angels, a volunteer group who organizes special patrols of the bridge to stop suicides and save lives.

Special Events

In the early stages of the advocacy effort, when the UC–Berkeley engineering students—then working with PFNC—produced scale models of suicide barriers, the UC–Berkeley press office saw an opportunity for a story. The result was promotion that brought extensive coverage of the students' work and visual representations of what could be tastefully done at the Golden Gate. From then on, advocates were able to organize special events and presentations to provide a dramatic visualization of the scale of suicides from the bridge, bring personal stories forward, demonstrate what a solution might look like, and attract press attention.

Among the most successful of these events was an idea developed based on the experience of one individual who witnessed an apparent suicide from the Golden Gate. Walking on the bridge one day, a Marin County architect noticed an abandoned pair of shoes placed neatly on the bridge sidewalk. He wondered whose shoes these might be and suspected they were left just before a jump over the short railing. There were no immediate answers to his questions, but he reported the incident and later passed the story along. The story of these abandoned shoes evoked much of the mystery and puzzlement surrounding bridge suicides and provided a perfect symbolic statement about the suicide problem. From this experience, the *Whose Shoes?* program by the Bridge Rail Foundation

FIGURE 4.2 A pair of shoes found abandoned on the Golden Gate Bridge was the inspiration for the *Whose Shoes?* exhibits organized by the Bridge Rail Foundation.

evolved. The foundation presented a number of *Whose Shoes?* exhibits over the years, including at a major public event to honor the 75th anniversary of the Golden Gate Bridge opening. These exhibits attracted tremendous press attention and delivered a powerful reminder of the ongoing tragedy. The story of the exhibit is described in more detail in the following chapter.

Image Credits

Persist! Advocacy and Engaging Decision Makers

In the spring of 2006, during the organizing for what would become the Bridge Rail Foundation, Pat Hines proposed an approach. Quite simply, he wanted to mobilize an "enraged constituency." Motivated by his own rage that his son Kevin had nearly died in a jump from the bridge and seeing the anger and pain expressed by many who had suffered a loss to bridge suicide, he pushed this approach as a winning strategy. Whereas many were indeed enraged, others were in a slow boil of anger, in a deep sense of mourning, or simply at a loss as to what to do. Hines was right. The survivor families—incensed at what befell their families, angered by the years of inaction at the most popular suicide spot in the world, and shocked by the mounting death toll—would bring to the effort a stubborn determination to see the suicides at the Golden Gate Bridge stop.

The Bridge District's past tactics to avoid dealing with the suicide problem included a slow approach to "reason" that pulled advocates into extended discussions of options and alternatives that led nowhere. There had been a barbed wire sample installed in the 1950s, architect sketches in the 1970s, and a dummy cattle fence displayed in the 1990s. These efforts absorbed all the time and energy put into creating a solution, which allowed the issue to fade and fizzle.

Pained, angry, and hurt surviving family members and friends would not get sucked into another plan-for-nothing trap. Despite the complexity of the engineering, funding, and political challenges ahead, what Pat Hines had described as "an enraged constituency" could provide something missing from previous advocacy efforts—persistence.

Friend or Foe?

The Bridge District was the problem. The district alone was in charge, and there was no reasonable means to proceed without changing the attitude it had held for decades. Yet, during the entire history of efforts at suicide prevention, there were always individuals within the district who sought to end the suicide problem. At the top—the district's board of directors—were some supporters, but they could never muster a majority of the 19-member board. And a board representing a diffuse geographic area and different constituencies was not likely to initiate building a suicide barrier. Compounding this was the fact that most of the board had little understanding of suicide and how it might be prevented. Indeed, previous efforts had been quite assertive in examining reasonable alternatives and pushing for a solution, but the board as a whole was simply not moved.

The district's senior staff leaders were also not moved. Their focus was on running a transportation system—the bridge, buses, and ferries. The landmark status of the bridge and its position as an international tourist attraction, roadway, bikeway, and pedestrian walkway were also primary concerns. Suicide was an unfortunate problem, but they would claim there was little they could do. Some staff members were, in fact, horrified at what they had learned of or witnessed during a bridge suicide. They may have spoken up internally, but the public knew little of their concern. In the end, there was simply no concerted effort to end the suicides or convince others to take on the issue.

As it turned out, two key individuals in leadership positions within the district—a board member and a senior staff member—would play a key role in getting the district to a place where construction would finally be approved. These were board member Tom Ammiano, a San Francisco supervisor and later state assemblyman, and Denis Mulligan, the chief engineer who was later promoted to general manager with the departure of Celia Kupersmith. However, these individuals could not have done so without the consistent prodding from outside advocates, principally the "enraged constituency." The challenge before this "constituency" was to move the district as a whole from foe to friend and ensure they stayed friendly.

Early Approvals

The plans the district called for in 2005 were presented in 2008. Five options were offered, including a suicide deterrent net system strung 20 feet below the bridge deck and extending out 20 feet on each side of the bridge. With the presentation of these plans, the district had a choice: they could designate the net system as the preferred option and order its environmental analysis and engineering studies, select one of four other options that featured taller railings, or go back to the drawing board. A critical vote was before the district, and advocates needed to ensure a positive outcome.

Bridge Rail volunteers went to work contacting the district's decision makers. Meetings, personal calls, and last-minute breakfast appointments were done before the hearing. During the hearing, many families spoke before the board, with a vision of a suicide prevention structure, at least on paper. Bridge Rail members organized detailed presentations to ensure the board and attending press had a complete picture of the problem and the research that supported construction. Mark Whitmer organized a presentation that included a detailed account of more than 20 years of research supporting access restriction to prevent suicides and the records of such successes on other bridges. Dayna Whitmer presented the Bridge District board with a petition signed by more than 450 individuals, many with personal notes about lost family and friends. Signers came from 35 states and elsewhere in North America, plus Europe, Asia, Africa, and Australia. She also presented a summary of the California Suicide Prevention Plan, which addressed access restriction and suicide prevention. Bridge Rail president Dave Hull presented a detailed letter from the National Suicide Prevention Lifeline—the organization representing U.S. suicide crisis lines—which also detailed the research support. Eve Meyer of SF Suicide Prevention spoke with specific reference to the previous efforts to stop suicide at the bridge and the subsequent inaction. Dr. Blaustein also spoke with the support of the local psychiatric community and the San Francisco Medical Society. Episcopalian and Presbyterian ministers went on record in support of the net, as did Catholic Social Services.

In addition to the established support for the net, advocates recognized the need for a response to those who might object to any physical structure added to the bridge. Much of the opposition had been mollified by the net proposal already because of its more acceptable aesthetics. Yet, one opponent—a university professor who was not at the public hearing—wrote a detailed attempt to refute the research Mark Whitmer and others had referred to. His letter to the Bridge District—on university letterhead—was an attempt to derail the proposal completely. A thorough response was needed. Anne Fleming, MD, an assistant clinical professor of psychiatry at University of California–San Francisco, joined with David Elkin, MD, a UCSF clinical professor, in an in-depth rebuttal. Dr. Fleming presented their paper to the bridge board at the hearing and pointed out a series of misrepresentations and mischaracterizations in the opponent's letter. Finally, to ensure that the magnitude of the bridge suicide problem was not missed, Marin coroner Ken Holmes appeared before the board with the raw statistics. With the actual body count and his deep experience at testifying in criminal trials, Holmes's presentation was not easy to refute. Following the hearing, the board voted to approve the suicide deterrent net as the preferred option. There was only one *no* vote.

The Bridge District vote in 2008 was a key turning point in the fight for a suicide barrier at the Golden Gate. For one thing, the board now had an established position favoring construction. This position, in turn, freed up—or required—district staff to pursue development of the net as official policy. The old foe was turning friendly, but the issue was far from resolved.

The Bridge Rail Foundation understood that the road ahead featured many complex twists and turns. Many decisions from within public agencies would have to be made, and the overall support the foundation had shown before the Bridge District would need to be replicated and reinforced throughout the coming years. And, of course, the project had to be funded.

Elected Officials

From the earliest efforts, Bridge Rail knew the importance of communication with federal elected officials on the project. Founding member Pat Hines had arranged a showing of Eric Steel's film for the Washington staff of Senator Barbara Boxer. We also knew that California's other senator, Dianne Feinstein, had lost a personal friend to suicide at Golden Gate. And both senators were known to support a suicide barrier when they served as bridge board members years earlier. In the House, Bridge Rail worked with the two members who had the bridge within their districts—Nancy Pelosi and Lynn Woolsey. Pelosi, of course, was House speaker or minority leader throughout the period Bridge Rail was active. The coroner's statistics that showed that over 80% of bridge suicides were from among Bay Area residents (see Chapter 2 sidebar). Thus, it was clear this problem affected every congressional district in the region. Congresswomen Pelosi and Woolsey began to circulate a letter of support, which was subsequently signed by every member of the House from the Bay Area (in fact, there were more signers—from Los Angeles and Chicago).

As a result, Bridge Rail was able to present to the Bridge District and transportation funding agencies a letter signed by all members of the Bay Area delegation insisting the problem be resolved. After the delivery of the letter, advocates took the opportunity to visit individual congressional offices to ensure local staff was aware of the project. A similar effort was made with state legislative officials, where occasional legislative initiatives supporting suicide prevention allowed the foundation to bring the story forward. Additionally, Bridge Rail met with legislators who had lost family members to suicide and were very supportive of its effort. As it turned out, funding the district's proposed suicide deterrent net was also dependent on a number of obscure changes in federal law. Senator Boxer was receptive to our efforts and—working directly with the Bridge District—included the needed language in a larger transportation bill working its way through the committee she chaired. In one of the more dysfunctional Congresses in recent years, this legislation passed the Senate and House and was signed by President Barack Obama in 2012.

Other than the Bridge District, the primary public entity with which Bridge Rail needed to communicate was the local transportation planning agency—MTC (Metropolitan Transportation Commission). This agency—composed mostly of local elected officials—had control over much of the highway construction funding and knew the funding cycle well. Thus, Bridge Rail also made regular appearances at the agency's formal public hearings. Foundation volunteers also spoke directly with members of the MTC board and staff to encourage their support. Within both the state legislature and transportation planning agency, Bridge Rail came across decision makers with family members who had died by suicide. These individuals understood more deeply the pain our members expressed.

The General Public

Bridge Rail advocates were eager to keep the fight in the public eye. Beyond the media coverage and formal advocacy at meetings, public events associated with other suicide prevention agencies, mental health programs, or similar meetings offered opportunities to reinforce the foundation's efforts and connect directly with friendly, supportive audiences.

Bridge Rail's most successful *Whose Shoes?* display was at a unique event. The Golden Gate Bridge would be 75 years old in May 2012, and the district planned a large community-wide celebration, also in the Crissy Field area. By this time, the district welcomed Bridge Rail as an exhibitor and assigned the foundation a display area to use as it saw fit. This location featured large L-shaped concrete blocks stepping up into the landscape of the west bluff. Bridge Rail covered the steps in black cloth and arranged more than 1,500 pairs of shoes on the display. Additionally, simple chalk outlines of 200 pairs of shoes were added throughout the display to represent individuals lost to suicide, whose bodies were never recovered. Surviving family members staffed the display wearing black t-shirts with the number 1,558 across the back to represent the total number of confirmed deaths as of that date.

FIGURE 5.1 Visitors take note of over 1,500 pairs of shoes representing the lives lost to suicide at the Golden Gate Bridge. This display was part of the 2012 event to commemorate the 75 years since the bridge opened.

Local print media again reported on the *Whose Shoes?* installation, as did radio and television stations. In addition to the local press, an Associated Press reporter took special interest and turned the event and its visual image into a national story. Many local papers across the country carried the wire story, which was accompanied by a great deal of supportive photography. The Golden Gate suicide issue—previously covered in depth in both the *Washington Post* and *New York Times*—would persist in the national consciousness through Bridge Rail efforts with the national media.

In addition, key supporters also kept the issue fresh on the national scene through an ongoing set of presentations. First among these was Kevin Hines, whose national speaking program on his experience surviving a Golden Gate Bridge suicide attempt continued to grow. A gifted and captivating speaker, Hines was and is a regular attraction before audiences, including university campuses, military assemblies, professional groups, and mental health organizations. In addition, Eric Steel continued to show *The Bridge* throughout the United States. Visual evidence of the horror at the bridge, the pain of surviving family members and friends, and the heroics others displayed became widespread.

Furthermore, *The Bridge* wasn't the only relevant film. Jenni Olsen released *The Joy of Life* in 2005. The film features stunning visuals against a narrative contemplation of suicide from the bridge, including a story of one woman's search for love and self-discovery. The award-winning film remains popular in festivals and art film houses.

John Brooks, whose daughter Casey died in a jump from the Golden Gate in 2008, became a frequent op-ed contributor and interviewee in the local press. Eventually, he also published *The Girl Behind the Door*, a memoir detailing his quest to understand his daughter's death. John was also readily available for interviews and maintained an active social media presence.

In 2012, John Bateson, then head of the Contra Costa Crisis Center, which provides suicide crisis call services for the county directly east of the Golden Gate Bridge, published *The Final Leap* with the University of California Press. Bateson's book, which includes a brief history of the Bridge Rail Foundation and the fight for a suicide barrier, also features many of the stories from surviving family members. Indeed, with important historical analysis and stories from families, first responders, and many others affected by suicide at the Golden Gate Bridge, his book has become a primary reference on the topic.

In 2013, BRF board member Dayna Whitmer cowrote "Analysis of the Cost Effectiveness of a Suicide Barrier on the Golden Gate Bridge," which was published in *Crisis*, 34(2), 98–106. It concluded that a suicide barrier on the Golden Gate Bridge would be highly cost-effective in reducing suicide mortality in the San Francisco Bay Area.

A strategy of persistence is very difficult to maintain in a voluntary, community-based organization. In fact, such a strategy had eluded several previous efforts to resolve the Golden Gate suicide problem. Yet, starting with the moment that news of Eric Steel's film would be released, a series of events, publications, presentations, and other films have kept the bridge suicide story going. In so doing, advocates could persist in their demands to stop the suicides at the bridge.

Persist—with Clear Goals

A suicide prevention program aimed at an identified deadly jumping site can state its goals very clearly. So it was with the effort at the Golden Gate begun in 2004 with the Psychiatric Foundation. In 2006, the Bridge Rail Foundation formally adopted the simple mission statement "Stop the suicides at the Golden Gate Bridge." This goal remained Bridge Rail's sole focus through the signing of the construction contract in 2017.

The process of getting the Bridge District to stop suicides at the Golden Gate was a complex undertaking. What we saw was then a multistep process involving evaluation, engineering, funding, and permitting needed before construction would actually start. The project could be stopped at any one of these steps. stopped at any one of these steps, including:

1. Ordering design proposals for a physical structure;

2. Evaluating and testing the proposals;

3. Gauging public reaction;

4. Approving a preferred preliminary design;

5. Ordering environmental analysis;

6. Contracting for detailed design and engineering;

7. Approval of final design;

8. Securing needed permits for construction;

9. Securing funding—from multiple sources;

10. Bidding the job;

11. Securing additional funds as needed; and

12. Accepting the low bid and signing the contract.

The necessity of each step would mean that each provided an important milestone as the project moved forward. Thus, advocates could understand how their advocacy was received—and if it was effective. From the advocates' point of view, these steps became critical evaluation points. Each hurdle that was overcome was distinct progress toward the goal of stopping suicides on the Golden Gate Bridge.

Understanding of the complexity of the process, advocates were also able to properly focus or adjust their program to best ensure reaching the goal. There were steps along the way that advocates could influence or effect and others where there was little opportunity for advocates or the general public to influence the progress.

Most important, of course, was the decision making at the Bridge District itself— specifically, ordering design proposals for the physical structure; approving a preferred preliminary design; approval of final design; and accepting the low bid and signing the contract. Failure at any one of these points would stop the effort again, likely resulting in many additional years before another effort was mounted. Still understanding the importance of these decision points meant advocates could focus advocacy better and strengthen the chance of success. Thus, as has been reported here, substantial efforts were mounted to persuade bridge board members to support each succeeding step along the path to approval. And following each successful approval, advocates were able to review the work that had been done and plan the approach needed for the next step.

Of course, there were elements in the approval process that were more technical in nature, about which advocates would have little influence. Bridge Rail understood this, but still took the position to double-check things whenever possible. For example, when the net system was first proposed, foundation volunteers carefully checked the claims of effectiveness, while knowing full well that this option had the most appeal to those concerned about any alteration to the bridge or the dramatic views from it. Once convinced of the effectiveness of a net system around Munster Terrace in Bern, Switzerland, support for the net proposal was an acceptable alternative. It did, however, carry additional risk, as the net would be a more costly project than any of the taller railing options. On this point, too, a careful evaluation of the options available was needed, and Bridge Rail concluded the net was the best option likely to see eventual approval.

The Bridge District approved the net as the preferred alternative on October 10, 2008. An environmental analysis was completed, and it was approved by the bridge board on February 12, 2010. The next steps, however, were very much an open question and involved a number of outside parties. Advocacy now would need to reach an additional set of decision makers, many with differing priorities. These would include the Metropolitan Transportation Commission (MTC), the Bay Conservation and Development Commission (BCDC), the National Park Service (NPS), the California Department of Transportation (CalTrans), and perhaps both houses of Congress. One major shift after the 2010 decision—the Bridge District now had a project it was officially pursuing, and Bridge District staff would now work directly supporting construction of the project they called the suicide deterrent net. At each succeeding step along the approval process, the Bridge District, too, would advocate for the project. Bridge Rail's job became much simpler— keeping the story of the tragedy before the public, encouraging the Bridge District to push forward, and ensuring that any outstanding objections could be met.

Image Credits

Fig. 5.1: Copyright © 2012 Bridge Rail Foundation/Cristina Taccone. Reprinted with permission.

6

Challenging and Refuting Misconceptions

It's important to note that because the stigma and shame long associated with suicide are buried deep within our culture, refuting misconceptions is a necessary component of advocacy efforts. Stigmatizing and shameful behaviors are generally not talked about. They are stuffed in the back and out of sight and the narrative or story can easily be incomplete and lead to misconceptions. When such a story is repeated enough to become the common explanation of events, it becomes a culturally ingrained "commonsense" view of the situation. When beliefs become culturally ingrained, getting people to accept a new way of thinking can be difficult. Just as Galileo was threatened by religious authorities for challenging the ingrained belief that the Earth, not the sun, was the center of the solar system, many in society ridicule the notion that suicides are preventable and that suicidal individuals are deserving of understanding and care rather than judgment and shaming.

Much of the research supporting a newer and more complete understanding of suicide was described earlier. But understanding popular assumptions in our culture and how they are presented was a major challenge to effective advocacy at the Golden Gate Bridge. Likewise, these ideas will continue to frustrate other suicide prevention efforts.

Statements such as, "if someone really wants to kill themselves, they will," "if you stop a suicide here, they will just go someplace else," or "it's their decision, their free will," are common in society, and many choose to believe these ideas as the prevailing wisdom on suicide. Yet, research into suicide and prevention approaches has either debunked these concepts thoroughly or illuminated how they represent a truth applicable to only a limited number of self-inflicted lethal injuries. The validity of these beliefs, if there is any, is quite small, but these concepts are deeply ingrained in the culture. The perpetuation of these false notions represented a significant challenge for efforts to stop suicides on the Golden Gate Bridge and continues to hamper suicide prevention efforts at other public sites, including bridges, rail systems, and tall cliffs.

There are examples of the influence of these misconceptions throughout history and in how they are reflected in artistic works, such as literature and theatre. Consider, for example, Shakespeare's character Hamlet. In his famous soliloquy, even as a ruse, Hamlet portrays himself pondering "to be or not to be." The question appears as a rational idea, the same as any thoughtful character might contemplate any other rational, thoughtful choice. Like much of Shakespeare, the play has remained popular and thus is performed repeatedly. To many, Hamlet's perspective represents what suicide is—a rational choice to consider. This sort of rationalization is also allocated to suicides of historical figures. For instance, the suicide of Adolf Hitler near the end of World War II is significant. He was responsible for starting the war and murdering millions, and when the Soviet Army overran Berlin, his only option was to surrender and throw himself at the mercy of Stalin. To many, he represents a classic "trapped rat" with no reasonable means of escape. Therefore, his suicide is understood as a rational choice. Again, this death provides a view of a suicide well known in society, yet it represents only a small fragment of the suicidal population. Hollywood—and other purveyors of popular culture—often present suicide as either a detached, rational choice or the only option for a person truly trapped. The problem is that whereas the Hamlet, Hitler, and popular Hollywood representations of suicide may ring true, such suicides account for a small percentage of suicide deaths. The cultural power of these stories has greatly enlarged their authority and contributed to a basic misunderstanding of suicide in general. This misunderstanding leaks into policy and politics; therefore, advocates are required to challenge these cultural assumptions or risk frustration and defeat.

To combat these messages, it is important to point to national strategies that include reducing access to lethal means as an important component in a comprehensive approach. The 2012 National Strategy for Suicide Prevention (the National Strategy) was the result of a joint effort by the Office of the U.S. Surgeon General and the National Action Alliance for Suicide Prevention (Action Alliance). The National Strategy set forth an ambitious agenda for suicide prevention, consisting of 11 goals and 68 objectives, to reflect advances in suicide prevention knowledge, research, and practice, as well as broader changes in society and health care delivery that have created new opportunities for suicide prevention.

National Strategy goals and objectives include the following:[1]

- ▷ A discussion of how suicide is related to mental illness, substance abuse, trauma, violence, and other related issues;

- ▷ Information on population groups that may be at an increased risk for suicidal behaviors;

- ▷ A review of interventions that may be most effective for suicide prevention; and

- ▷ A recognition of the importance of implementing suicide prevention efforts in a comprehensive and coordinated way.

Within the public health sphere, any comprehensive prevention plan addresses primary, secondary, and tertiary interventions. Primary prevention refers to intervening before negative health effects occur through measures such as vaccinating, altering risky behaviors (e.g., poor eating habits, tobacco use), and banning substances known to be associated with a disease or health conditions.[2] Secondary prevention involves screening to identify diseases in the earliest stages before the onset of signs and symptoms through measures such as mammography and regular blood pressure testing.[3] Tertiary prevention requires managing disease post-diagnosis to slow or stop disease progression

---

1   U.S. Department of Health and Human Services (HHS) Office of the Surgeon General and National Action Alliance for Suicide Prevention. (2012). Strategic direction 1: Healthy and empowered individuals, families, and communities. https://www.ncbi.nlm.nih.gov/books/NBK109907/

2   Wallace, R. B. (2006). [cited 2010 Mar. 30]. Primary prevention. In L. Breslow and G. Cengage (eds.), *Encyclopedia of Public Health* [online]. http://www.enotes.com/public-health- encyclopedia/primary-prevention

3   Wallace, R. B. (2006). [cited 2010 Mar. 30]. Secondary prevention. In L. Breslow and G. Cengage (eds.), *Encyclopedia of Public Health* [online]. http://www.enotes.com/public-health- encyclopedia/secondary-prevention

through measures such as chemotherapy, rehabilitation, and screening for complications.[4]

In response to the National Strategy, the Suicide Prevention Resource Center (SPRC) conceived of a comprehensive approach to suicide prevention and mental health promotion. The SPRC plan includes broad goals to advance the mission to reduce the number of suicides to zero through an array of activities described below. The explicit goal of eliminating suicide is set forth. The SPRC plan also clearly identifies programs to reduce access to lethal means as a key element to a comprehensive strategy for suicide prevention. Understanding the overall strategy for suicide prevention and how an advocacy program for bridge barriers, safer railings, or net systems is included is an important perspective for advocates. Not only does this knowledge position the advocate squarely within accepted national priorities, but it also helps identify potential allies currently working in other aspects of suicide prevention.[5]

Suicide Prevention Resource Center Comprehensive Suicide Prevention Approach

Train People to Identify and Assist Persons at Risk

Many people in distress don't seek help or support on their own. Identifying people at risk for suicide can help you reach those in the greatest need and connect them to care and support. Examples of activities in this strategy include gatekeeper training, suicide screening, and teaching warning signs.

Increase Help-Seeking

By teaching people to recognize when they need support—and helping them to find it—you can enable them to reduce their suicide risk. Self-help tools and outreach campaigns are examples of ways to lower an individual's barriers to obtaining help, such as not knowing what services exist or believing that help won't be effective. Other interventions might address the social and structural environment by, for example, fostering peer norms that support help-seeking or making services more convenient and culturally appropriate.

4   Wallace, R. B. (2006). [cited 2010 Mar. 30]. Tertiary prevention. In L. Breslow and G. Cengage (eds.), *Encyclopedia of Public Health* [online]. http://www.enotes. com/public-health-encyclo- pedia/tertiary-prevention

5   Suicide Prevention Resource Center. (2020). A comprehensive approach to suicide prevention. http://www.sprc.org/effective-prevention/comprehensive-approach

Ensure Access to Effective Mental Health and Suicide Care and Treatment

A key element of suicide prevention is ensuring that individuals with suicide risk have timely access to evidence-based treatments, suicide prevention interventions, and coordinated systems of care. Suicide prevention interventions such as safety planning and evidence-based treatments and therapies delivered by trained providers can lead to significant improvement and recovery. SPRC encourages health and behavioral health care systems to adopt the Zero Suicide framework for integrating these approaches into their systems. Reducing financial, cultural, and logistical barriers to care is another important strategy for ensuring access to effective mental health and suicide care treatment.

Support Safe Care Transitions and Create Organizational Linkages

You can reduce patients' suicide risk by ensuring that they have an uninterrupted transition of care and by facilitating the exchange of information among the various individuals and organizations that contribute to their care. Individuals at risk for suicide and their support networks (e.g., families) must also be part of the communication process. Tools and practices that support continuity of care include formal referral protocols, interagency agreements, cross-training, follow-up contacts, rapid referrals, and patient and family education.

Respond Effectively to Individuals in Crisis

Individuals in your school, organization, or community who are experiencing severe emotional distress may need a range of services. A full continuum of care includes not only hotlines and helplines but also mobile crisis teams, walk-in crisis clinics, hospital-based psychiatric emergency services, and peer-support programs. Crisis services directly address suicide risk by providing evaluation, stabilization, and referrals to ongoing care.

Provide for Immediate and Long-Term Postvention

A postvention plan is a set of protocols to help your organization or community respond effectively and compassionately to a suicide death. Immediate responses focus on supporting those affected by the suicide death and reducing risk to other vulnerable individuals. Postvention efforts should also include intermediate and long-term supports for people bereaved by suicide.

Reduce Access to Means of Suicide

One important way to reduce the risk of death by suicide is to prevent individuals in suicidal crisis from obtaining and using lethal methods of self-harm. Examples of actions to reduce access to lethal means include educating the families of those in crisis about safely storing medications and firearms, distributing gun safety locks, changing medication packaging, and installing barriers on bridges.

Enhance Life Skills and Resilience

By helping people build life skills, such as critical thinking, stress management, and coping, you can prepare them to safely address challenges like economic stress, divorce, physical illness, and aging. Resilience—the ability to cope with adversity and adapt to change—is a protective factor against suicide risk. While it has some overlap with life skills, resilience also encompasses other attributes, such as optimism, positive self-concept, and the ability to remain hopeful. Skills training, mobile apps, and self-help materials are examples of ways to increase life skills and build resilience.

Promote Social Connectedness and Support

Supportive relationships and community connectedness can help protect individuals against suicide despite the presence of risk factors in their lives. You can enhance connectedness through social programs for specific population groups (such as older adults or LGBT youth) and through other activities that reduce isolation, promote a sense of belonging, and foster emotionally supportive relationships.

Source: Suicide Prevention Resource Center, "A Comprehensive Approach to Suicide Prevention." Copyright © by Education Development Center, Inc. Reprinted with permission.

FIGURE 6.1 Signs installed above phones on the Golden Gate Bridge had little or no effect in reducing the suicides from the span.

Means Restriction: The Evidence

Challenging popular misconceptions requires becoming comfortable referencing national and regional public health trends and/or citing the empirical literature around reducing access to lethal means. For social workers and community advocates alike, searching for and interpreting the most relevant literature can be a daunting task.

The Wrong Direction

Despite unprecedented efforts and national strategies in suicide prevention, U.S. rates of suicide deaths have remained intractable over time. Over the past 50 years, global suicides have increased 60%, and between 1999 and 2016, the rates rose in all but one state, with increases seen across age, gender, race, and ethnicity. Further, the highest increases in suicide rates have been in largely rural states.[6] In North Dakota, for example, the rate jumped more than 57%. In the most recent period studied (2014 to 2016), the rate was highest in Montana, at 29.2 per 100,000 residents, compared to the national average of 13.4 per 100,000. Only Nevada recorded a decline of 1% during the overall period; however, its rate remained higher than the national average. The nature of this widespread increase makes it clear that this is a national problem hitting communities hard.

It is not uncommon for the topic of societal ills and systemic barriers to be correlated with the suicide problem. Life stressors, such as those involving work or finances, substance use problems, physical health conditions, or recent or impending personal crises, play a large role in a person's decision to take their life. Professionals in the fields of mental health, economy, sociology, and epidemiology have suggested that one factor for the noted increased rates is the Great Recession that hit the nation in 2008.[7] In fact, a 2017 study in the academic journal *Social Science and Medicine* provided evidence that a rise in the foreclosure rate during that concussive downturn was associated with an overall, though marginal, increase in suicide rates. The increase was higher for White males than any other race or gender group. The dramatic rise in opioid

---

6   Ingraham, C. (2018, May, 24). Mapping the rising tide of suicide deaths across the United States. *The Washington Post.*

7   Strumpf, E. C., Charters, T. J., Harper, S., & Nandi, A. (2017). Did the Great Recession affect mortality rates in the metropolitan United States? Effects on mortality by age, gender and cause of death. *Social Science & Medicine*, Vol. 189, pp. 11–16. ISSN 0277-9536.

addiction also cannot be overlooked, but untangling accidental from intentional deaths by overdose can be difficult. Opioid overdoses nearly doubled between 1999 and 2014, and data from a 2014 national survey showed that individuals addicted to prescription opioids had a 40%–60% higher risk of suicidal ideation. Habitual opioid users were twice as likely to attempt suicide as people who did not use them.[8] Finally, suicide among women has also increased. Historically, men have had higher death rates than women, but those numbers have equalized, not from a decline in men's suicides, but from an escalation of suicides among women.[9]

A high number of suicides are among people with no diagnosed mental health condition. In the 27 states that use the National Violent Death Reporting System, 54% of suicides fell into this category. The problem is that when a psychological autopsy is performed on these individuals, wherein their medical records are examined and family members interviewed, as many as 90% of them will show evidence of a mental health condition.[10] So, why is there a large portion of people going undiagnosed? Cultural attitudes may play a part. Those without a diagnosed mental health condition were more likely to be male and also belong to a racial or ethnic minority group.

The lack of confirmed diagnosis and continuous treatment is often due to systemic barriers of the strained and even fractured American mental health care system. Stingy insurance authorizations, which are required (even daily reauthorization), are needlessly time consuming for already overburdened hospitals, doctors, and staff.[11]

Effective prevention strategies include responsible media coverage, general public education, screening, gatekeeper training, and—the two most well-established strategies—primary care physician intervention and restricted access to lethal means.[12]

---

8   Bohnert, A. S., & Ilgen, M. A. (2019). Understanding links among opioid use, overdose, and suicide. *New England Journal of Medicine, 380*(1), 71–79.

9   Monaco, K. (2018, June 14). Suicide rate in women jumps by 50%—From 2000–2016, rates also increased by 21% in men. *MedPage Today.*

10   National Center for Injury Prevention and Control, Division of Violence Prevention. (2019, Nov. 7). National Violent Death Reporting System (NVDRS). Center for Disease Control and Prevention. https://www.cdc.gov/violencepreven-tion/datasources/nvdrs/index.html?CDC_AA_refVal=https%3A%2F%2Fwww.cdc.gov%2Fviolenceprevention%2Fnvdrs%2Findex.html

11   Tessier, M. (2018, June 13). 6 Therapists, psychiatrists and counselors talk about treating the suicidal. *New York Times.*

12   Schwartz-Lifshitz, M., Zalsman, G., Giner, L., & Oquendo, M. A. (2012). Can we really prevent suicide? *Current Psychiatry Reports, 14*(6), 624–633.

Reducing Access to Lethal Means

Means restriction, or reducing a suicidal person's access to lethal means, is an acknowledged part of comprehensive strategies on suicide prevention but may not be getting enough focused attention. The National Strategy on Suicide Prevention (2012) and most state suicide prevention plans call for reducing access to lethal means, finding that means restriction is an "effective strategy to prevent self-destructive behaviors in certain individuals."[13] Moreover, an international panel of suicide prevention experts reviewed the research literature in 2005 and concluded that means restriction was one of only two suicide prevention strategies that was considered evidence based.[14]

The rationale for reducing a suicidal person's access to lethal means is simple—the urge toward suicide can pass over time and lives can be saved. Consider, for example a study on teenagers and young adults (13–34

FIGURE 6.2 Pedestrians on the east side walkway of the Golden Gate Bridge clearly demonstrate the short original railing.

---

13   The Action Alliance. (2020). National Strategy for Suicide Prevention. https://theactionalliance.org/our-strategy/national-strategy-suicide-prevention

14   Beautrais, A., Fergusson, D., Coggan, C., et.al. (2007, March 23). Effective strategies for suicide prevention in New Zealand: A review of evidence. *N Z Med J. 120*(1251): U245.

years old) that examined how much time passed between the moment they decided on the suicide and the attempt. Twenty-five percent said it was less than 5 minutes. Many of the others started to think about attempting suicide within 5–10 minutes of the attempt.[15] Additionally, acute suicidal phases are often brief, and the acute period of heightened risk for suicidal behavior is often only minutes or hours long.

Most people who consider suicide feel ambivalent about ending their own life. Their determination of suicidal feelings comes and goes. Unfortunately, bridge jumps, like firearms, don't allow for an individual to change their mind or be rescued. There is no turning back. Therefore, if highly lethal means are not available, an individual may delay the attempt or use a less lethal means, which would allow for more opportunities to be rescued. For example, most people likely think that pills and razors are deadly means of suicide, but these misperceptions actually save lives because these types of attempts are often reversible, meaning they involve a small window in which the person can back out or be saved. And we know 9 of 10 people who survive a suicide attempt do not die by suicide at a later date.

The suicidology literature has also established that individuals who survive suicides often do not die in subsequent attempts. A literature review conducted by Owens and colleagues in 2002 summarized 90 studies that followed people who made suicide attempts that resulted in medical care.[16] Of all those followed, approximately 7% (range of 5%–11%) did eventually die by suicide, approximately 23% reattempted nonfatally, and 70% made no further attempts.[17] Even studies that focused on highly lethal attempts, such as people who jumped in front of a train[18] as well as studies that followed attempters for many decades, found similarly low

---

15   Deisenhammer, E. A., Ing, C. M., Strauss, R., Kemmler, G., Hinterhuber, H., & Weiss, E. M. (2009). The duration of the suicidal process: How much time is left for intervention between consideration and accomplishment of a suicide attempt? *Journal of Clinical Psychiatry, 70*(1), 19–24. Milner, A. J., Lee, M. D., & Nock, M. K. (2017). Describing and measuring the pathway to suicide attempts: A preliminary study. *Suicide and Life-Threatening Behavior, 47*(3), 353–369.

16   Owens, D., Horrocks, J., & House, A. (2002). Fatal and non-fatal repetition of self-harm: Systematic review. *British Journal of Psychiatry 181*: 193–199.

17   Carroll, R., Metcalfe, C., & Gunnell, D. (2014). Hospital presenting self-harm and risk of fatal and non-fatal repetition: Systematic review and meta-analysis. PLoS ONE 9(2): e89944. https://doi.org/10.1371/journal.pone.0089944

18   O'Donnell, I., Arthur, A., & Farmer, R. (1994). A follow-up study of attempted railway suicides. *Social Science and Medicine, 38*: 437–442.

suicide completion rates. This relatively good long-term survival rate is consistent with the observation that suicidal crises are often short-lived, even if there may be underlying, more chronic risk factors present that give rise to these crises.

Especially in areas with suicidal hotspots, the limiting of access that makes it difficult to perform suicidal acts is effective in reducing suicides, as one recent systematic review suggested.[19] Evidence also suggests that restricting access to lethal means at one site does not drive suicidal individuals to seek alternative locations, thereby shifting the problem elsewhere. There are also indications that reducing suicides by a particular method does not lead to a substitution in suicide methods.

The effectiveness of installing barriers at suicide hotspots is consistent with the broader literature on restricting access to means as a population-level suicide prevention strategy. Indeed, research suggests that this strategy is one of very few universal prevention approaches for which there is strong evidence of effectiveness. Means reduction is an important part of a comprehensive approach to reduce a suicidal person's access to dangerous and highly effective methods.

Jumping from Bridges

As previously discussed, the largest issues surrounding jumping from a great height are that the act is highly lethal and nonreversible. Some communities have erected barriers at popular suicide jump sites. Barriers have been largely effective in stopping or dramatically reducing suicide deaths from that jump spot. But, the question remains, is there a commensurate increase in deaths by other methods? Some studies have found no increase; one study found some evidence of an increase for males only; and others either did not examine this aspect or did not have enough statistical power to examine it (since jumps do not make up a large proportion of suicides in most areas). Most studies have found that erecting a barrier does not result in more jumps from nearby sites.

To make a case for supporting a reduction of access to bridges as a lethal means, becoming familiar with the empirical literature is important. The Harvard Injury Control Research Center, which is part of the Harvard School of Public Health, provides a comprehensive summary of the research.[20]

19   Cox, G. R., Owens, C., Robinson, J., Nicholas, A., Lockley, A., Williamson, M., Cheung, Y. T., & Pirkis, J. (2013). Interventions to reduce suicides at suicide hotspots: a systematic review. BMC public health, 13, 214.

20   Harvard Injury Control Research Center. (2020). Suicide, guns, and public health. https://www.hsph.harvard.edu/means-matter/

Accessibility and Efficacy of Barriers

In 2004, a study was reported by Lindqvist and colleagues in Sweden that analyzed a sequential community-based case series of 50 individuals who committed suicide by jumping from bridges in two regions of Sweden. Of the 50 subjects, 32 were men and 18 were women (median age 35 years). At least 40 had psychiatric problems. The summer months and weekends saw the highest frequency of suicide. A total of 27 bridges were used. Almost half of all the suicides occurred from three bridges. Because this study demonstrated that few bridges attracted suicide candidates, the authors recommended that road system owners need to acknowledge this injury mechanism and include it in safety work.[21]

A higher prevalence of suicide by jumping was found when a suitable location was more accessible. According to Beautrais (2007), the incidence of suicide by jumping varies but tends to be higher in jurisdictions that have extensive high-rise housing.[22] Most incidents occur from high-rise residential housing units. However, our knowledge about suicide by jumping tends to be limited to a small number of reports from sites, often bridges. Poorly crafted media reports from these sites appear to encourage imitative behavior. Prevention strategies have focused on limiting suicides from iconic sites by surveillance, barriers, muted media reporting, and signage offering help and telephone hotlines. Evidence from these studies shows that installing physical barriers at popular jumping sites reduces suicides.

Authors have also published results regarding increases in suicide when means are accessible. Lin and Lu (2006), in an ecological study in Taiwan, explored the association between the accessibility to lethal methods and method-specific suicide rates. The authors calculated suicide rates for 5 years within 23 counties and cities and, when adjusting for unemployment and depression rates, found a strong positive correlation (0.77) between rurality and poisoning, as well as between suicide by jumping and living on or above the sixth floor (0.73). Hanging rates were not related to the proportion of agricultural households or the proportion of households living on or above the sixth floor. The

21 Lindqvist, P., Jonsson, A., Eriksson, A., Hedelin, A., & Björnstig, U. (2004). Are suicides by jumping off bridges preventable? An analysis of 50 cases from Sweden. *Accid Anal Prev, 36*(4): 691–694.

22 Beautrais, A. (2007). Suicide by jumping: A review of research and prevention strategies. *Crisis: The Journal of Crisis Intervention and Suicide Prevention*: 28(Suppl 1): 58–63.

authors concluded that because localities with little access to pesticides (the leading poisoning method) and tall buildings were no more likely to have a higher rate of suicide by hanging (a universally available method); restricting pesticide availability and adding barriers to high places in localities that do may help prevent suicides.[23]

Among bridges identified as hotspots that had barriers erected, Bennewith and colleagues (2007) studied the local pattern of suicides at a suspension bridge in England. The authors assessed the effect of the 1998 installation of barriers on the Clifton Suspension Bridge in Bristol on local suicides by jumping. Deaths from this bridge halved from 8.2 per year (1994–1998) to 4.0 per year (1999–2003). Although males constituted 90% of the suicides from the bridge, no evidence was found of an increase in male suicide by jumping from other sites in the Bristol area once barriers had been erected. This study provides evidence for the effectiveness of barriers on bridges in preventing site-specific suicides and suicides by jumping overall in the surrounding area.[24]

Naturalistic experimental testing was implemented by Cantor and Hill (1990) during the opening of a high river bridge in Brisbane, Australia. The researchers studied whether the sample engaging in suicidal behavior from the new bridge was similar to that from the adjoining older bridge. The differences in rate of suicide from these two bridges were substantial.[25] This suggests that persons prevented from jumping from one bridge, for example by a barrier, will not automatically jump from the alternative bridge, although a minority may do so.

In 2001, Beautrais reported on a case study to discuss the effectiveness of barriers at suicide jumping sites. After having been in place for 60 years, suicide safety barriers were removed from a central city bridge in an Australasian metropolitan area in 1996. A known suicide site, the bridge is located adjacent to the region's largest hospital, which includes an acute inpatient psychiatric unit. Removal of safety barriers led to an immediate and substantial increase in both the numbers and rate of suicides by jumping from the bridge in question. In the 4 years

23   Lin, J., & Lu, T. (2006). Association between the accessibility to lethal methods and method-specific suicide rates: An ecological study in Taiwan. *J Clin Psychiatry, 67*(7): 1074–1079.

24   Bennewith, O., Nowers, M., & Gunnell, D. (2007). Effect of barriers on the Clifton Suspension Bridge, England, on local patterns of suicide: Implications for prevention. *Br J Psychiatry,* 190: 266–267.

25   Cantor, C. H., & Hill, M. A. (1990). Suicide from river bridges. *Aust N Z J Psychiatry,* 3: 377–380.

FIGURE 6.3 BRF president Dave Hull and Jean Hull staff an outreach table at the annual AFSP fund-raising walk.

after the removal (compared with the previous 4 years), the number of suicides increased from 3 to 15. Young male psychiatric patients with psychotic illnesses composed the majority of those who died by jumping from the bridge. Following the removal of the barriers from the bridge, there were more suicides occurring from the bridge in question and fewer at other sites.[26]

Similarly, in 2009, Beautrais and colleagues published another case report about safety barriers to prevent suicide by jumping being removed from Grafton Bridge in Auckland, New Zealand. After having been in place for 60 years, the barriers were reinstalled in 2003. This study compared mortality data for suicide deaths for three time periods: 1991–1995 (old barrier in place); 1997–2002 (no barriers in place); and 2003–2006 (new barriers in place). Removal of barriers was followed by a fivefold increase in the number and rate of suicides from the bridge. Since the reinstallation of barriers, there have been no suicides from the bridge.[27]

26   Beautrais, A. (2001). Effectiveness of barriers at suicide jumping sites: A case study. *Australian and New Zealand Journal of Psychiatry, 35*(5): 557–562.

27   Beautrais, A., Gibb, S., Fergusson, D., Horwood, L. J., & Larkin, G. L. (2009). Removing bridge barriers stimulates suicides: An unfortunate natural experiment. *Australian and New Zealand Journal of Psychiatry, 43*(6): 495–497.

This natural experiment showed that safety barriers are effective in preventing suicide: their removal increases suicides; their reinstatement prevents suicides.

Substitution Fallacy

The belief in the inevitability of suicide through substitution methods was documented by Miller and colleagues in 2006. To examine public opinion regarding the effectiveness of means restriction as an approach to preventing suicide, the authors asked a national sample of 2,770 respondents a hypothetical question about what effect a suicide barrier might have ultimately had on the fate of the more than 1,000 people who have jumped to their death from the Golden Gate Bridge. Thirty-four percent of respondents believed that every single jumper would have found another way to complete the suicide, and an additional 40% believed that "most" would have done so.[28] The strongest predictors of belief in complete substitution were firearm ownership and cigarette smoking. This belief in the inevitability of suicide may be a political impediment to adopting suicide prevention efforts.

The theory of substitution methods has been demonstrated to be incorrect multiple times.[29] In 1978, in a follow-up study on the Golden Gate Bridge, a lack of substitution was observed. This research tested this contention by evaluating the long-term mortality of the 515 people who attempted suicide from the Golden Gate Bridge but were restrained from opening day through 1971, plus a comparison group of 184 persons who made non-bridge suicide attempts between 1956 and 1957 and were treated at an emergency department and then followed until the end of 1971. The author found that only about 10% of attempters went on to die by suicide.[30]

According to O'Carroll and Silverman (1994), the number one jump site in Washington, D.C., used to be the Ellington Bridge. In 1986, an

---

28   Miller, M., Azrael, D., & Hemenway, D. (2006). Belief in the inevitability of suicide: Results from a national survey. *Suicide Life Threatening Behavior, 36*(1): 1–11.

29   Daigle, M. (2005). Suicide prevention through means restriction: Assessing the risk of substitution. *Accident Analysis and Prevention, 37*(4), 625–632. https://doi.org/10.1016/j.aap.2005.03.004

30   Seiden, R. (1978). Where are they now? A follow-up study of suicide attempters from the Golden Gate Bridge. *Suicide and Life-Threatening Behavior, 8*(4), 203–20316.

8-ft. fence was erected as a barrier. In the 5 years that followed, there was no significant increase in suicide by jumping from the nearby Taft Bridge, and there was a reduction in suicide by jumping overall compared with figures from 1979 to 1985. The mean number of total suicides per year in Washington, D.C., decreased years before the barrier in the 5 years since.[31]

Similar results were replicated in 2007 by Pelletier. The author evaluated the effect on suicides of installing a bridge safety fence on the Memorial Bridge in Augusta, Maine, in 1983. From April 1, 1960, to July 31, 2005, there were 14 suicides from the bridge, all of which occurred before installation of the safety fence; afterward, there were zero suicides. The number of suicides by jumping from other structures remained unchanged after installation of the fence. The authors concluded that the safety fence was effective in preventing suicides from the bridge, and no evidence was found that suicidal individuals sought alternative sites for jumping.

Between 2005 and 2008, Reisch and Michel conducted three studies related to the effects of a safety net at the Bern Munster Terrace. The authors analyzed suicides by jumping before and after the installation of the net and assessed the number of media reports referring to this suicide method. No suicides occurred from the terrace after the installation of the net. Compared with the pre-installation period, the number of people jumping from all high places in Bern was significantly lower, indicating that no immediate shift to other nearby jumping sites took place. There was a moderate correlation between the number of media reports and the number of residents from outside Bern committing suicide by jumping from high places. In the second study, the researchers compared suicide data from regions with and without suicide bridges to estimate the effects on method and site substitution if bridges were to be secured. Suicide data for the years 1990–2003 were collected in a national survey. The analysis revealed that in regions with high rates of bridge suicides, compared with regions with low rates, about one third of the individuals would be expected to jump from buildings or other structures if no bridge was available. These results showed no substitution of method for women, but for men, a trend of substituting jumping by overdosing in regions without suicide bridges was found.

---

31   O'Carroll, P. W., & Silverman, M. M. (1994). Community suicide prevention: The effectiveness of bridge barriers. *Suicide and Life Threatening Behavior, 24*(1): 89–91; discussion 91–9.

In their last study, the researchers documented the psychiatric diagnostic characteristics, age, and gender of persons who ended their lives by jumping from heights and compared those who jumped from bridges with those who jumped from other sites. Persons who jumped from heights were more likely to be living with schizophrenia than those who used other methods. Persons who jumped from bridges were younger than those committing suicide by other methods. Subjects were on average 14.3 years younger and more often male compared with those who jumped from other sites. Individuals who jumped from bridges close to psychiatric hospitals were more likely to be diagnosed with a psychiatric illness.[32]

Two more recent studies retrospectively examined the impact of restricting access through temporary closures of sites. Skegg and Herbison (2009) studied the temporary closure of a jumping hotspot due to construction work. This scenario created an opportunity to assess whether loss of vehicular access would lead to a reduction in suicides and emergency police callouts for threatened suicide at the site. Using records from the local police inquest officer, the coroner's pathologist, and marine search and rescue, the study compared deaths during a 10-year period before and a two-year period after the road closure. Police data on the number of callouts for threatened suicide at the site were also compared with a 4-year period before and a 2-year period after the closure. There were 13 deaths involving suicide or open verdicts in the 10 years before access was restricted and none in the 2 years following closure. No jumping suicides occurred elsewhere in the police district after the road closure. Police callouts for threatened suicide also fell significantly, from 19.3 per year in the 4 years before to 9.5 per year for the following 2 years. Preventing vehicular access to a suicide jumping hotspot was an effective means of suicide prevention at the site. There was no evidence of substitution of other jumping sites.[33]

In 2010, Sinyor and Levitt compared 9 years of data on suicide by jumping before a barrier was installed at the Bloor Street Viaduct, a double-decked arch bridge in Toronto, Ontario, Canada, to 4 years of data afterward. Whereas the barrier was successful in preventing suicides, the rate of suicide by jumping in the region did not decline overall. There

32   Reisch, T., Schuster, U., & Michel, K. (2008). Suicide by jumping from bridges and other heights: Social and diagnostic factors. *Psychiatry Research*, *161*(1): 97–104.

33   Skegg, K., & Herbison, P. (2009). Effect of restricting access to a suicide jumping site. *Australian and New Zealand Journal of Psychiatry*, *43*(6): 498–502.

was a significant rise in suicide by jumping from nearby bridges. The authors concluded that installation of a barrier on one bridge may not alter the jump suicide rate if equally suitable jump sites are nearby.[34] In 2017, however, the research was refuted with the discovery that suicides have not increased at other bridges in the area.[35]

Clinical Approaches: Counseling on Reducing Access to Lethal Means (CALM)

While the focus of this book is on advocacy campaigns and community organizing to reduce access to lethal means, the process is often long and arduous. Clinically, an evidence-based intervention, Counseling on Access to Lethal Means, or CALM, addresses the nature of suicide attempts and encourages the reduction of access to lethal means until it is unavailable. This intervention is often not taught in social work or counseling programs despite its effectiveness. Because escalation of a suicidal crisis can happen rapidly, the goal is to make the home or environment safer for individuals at risk. People who have recently had suicidal thoughts, have attempted suicide in the past, are currently in distress, live with mental health or substance abuse issues, or are coping with a life crisis may have their lives saved through an access restriction intervention.[36] The intervention includes using collaborative, client-centered interventions to develop specific and feasible plans. In addition, the use of motivational interviewing helps gain input from the clients about reasons for and against increasing their safety. Necessary clinical steps include the following:

- Asking about suicidal thoughts and past suicide attempts, and asking direct questions and obtaining specific information is also important;

---

34 Sinyor, M., & Levitt, A. J. (2010). Effect of a barrier at Bloor Street Viaduct on suicide rates in Toronto: A natural experiment. *British Medical Journal, 340*: c2884.
35 Sinyor, M., Schaffer, A., Redelmeier, D. A., Kiss, A., et al. (2017). Did the suicide barrier work after all? Revisiting the Bloor Viaduct natural experiment and its impact on suicide rates in Toronto. *BMJ Open, 7*(5), e015299.
36 Education Development Center. (2014). Assessing and managing suicide risk: Core competencies for behavioral health professionals. [Participant companion guide]. Waltham, MA: Education Development Center.

- Asking about access to means, including methods of harm they have considered, and what access to lethal means they have in an impulsive moment; and

- Working with the suicidal individual and their family to restrict access.

A plan that identifies roles, timelines, and monitoring of progress is critical. Clinical documentation should include access to lethal means, plans for reducing access, and contacts with others, such as family members, law enforcement, pharmacy, or others, to hold or dispose of lethal means. Follow-up should include calls to check on progress, monitoring of suicide risk, making changes to the plan where necessary, and encouraging family or friends to closely supervise the at-risk individual.

Image Credits

Evaluating Suicide Prevention Programs

According to the Suicide Prevention Resource Center (2015), the first National Strategy for Suicide Prevention was released by Surgeon General David Satcher in 2001. Before then, the most successful prevention program was a U.S. Air Force effort in the 1990s, which involved a broad population-based approach that emphasized leadership, community education, improved health care, and surveillance. The results of this effort showed a 33% reduction in suicides between 1996 and 2002, with simultaneous reductions in homicide and family violence.[1]

The initial 2001 National Strategy emphasized public health methods, such as increasing awareness, reducing access to lethal means, providing better access to mental health care, and reducing the stigma of seeking such care. The next decade after the new strategy brought expanded suicide prevention efforts, including the Garrett Lee Smith Memorial Act of 2004, which created a youth suicide prevention grant program for states, colleges, and Native American/Alaska Native communities funded by the Substance Abuse and Mental Health Services Administration (SAMHSA). Many grantees emphasized risk screening, strengthening community partnerships, and building awareness for suicide warning signs in schools and communities by training frontline personnel to identify and refer at-risk youth to care. The counties that implemented these activities experienced fewer suicide attempts and deaths among youth compared with counties where the strategies were

---

1   Suicide Prevention Resource Center. (2015). *Challenges and recommendations for evaluating suicide prevention programs: State and tribal evaluators community of learning.* Waltham, MA: Education Development Center.

not implemented. However, the observed reductions were only among the target youth population and did not continue after the programs ended, which suggests that broader and more sustained efforts are needed.

Other national efforts included the establishment of a technical assistance center (the Suicide Prevention Resource Center) and a crisis call system—the National Suicide Prevention Lifeline. In 2007, the Department of Veterans Affairs established suicide protocols for its facilities and now supports a national hotline for veterans in crisis thru the Lifeline. This hotline has received nearly 2 million calls and dispatched emergency services for more than 56,000 veterans. Yet, despite these efforts, the number and rate of suicide deaths continue to rise.

The suicide rate of veterans aged 18 to 34 steadily increased from 2006 to 2016, with a jump of more than 10% from 2015 to 2016. This translates into 45 deaths per 100,000 veterans—the highest of any age group. Yet, since most veterans are older, most suicides occur among older veterans. Nearly 60% of veteran suicides in 2016 were by individuals 55 years or older.

Evaluating Suicide Prevention

Funding from public sources (approximately $40 million per year from the National Institutes of Health) state governments and private sources (approximately $20 million from the American Foundation for Suicide Prevention since 2002) for prevention programs and research has been prioritized in the past decade.

In general, suicide prevention programs include the following:

- Postvention responses for survivors to prevent future suicides;
- Crisis hotlines that provide immediate support and referral to care;
- Gatekeeper training for friends, family, clergy, and employees to learn how to identify signs of distress and refer to care;
- Marketing and outreach campaigns to create public awareness of suicidal risks and services available;

- Mental health interventions and therapeutic services delivered by mental health providers, including peer support programs;

- Medical provider training to improve awareness, risk assessment, and management;

- Screening programs that identify and refer at-risk individuals through the use of standardized instruments;

- Coping skills development for at-risk individuals; and

- Means restriction or modifications to the physical environment.

FIGURE 7.1 Retired Marin coroner Ken Holmes at a January 2014 press conference to announce the 48 suicide deaths from the bridge in the previous year. In the background are surviving family members holding pictures of loved ones lost to suicide at the Golden Gate.

Evaluation Challenges

With all of the various programs to address the problem of suicide, one would expect greater success. However, evaluation of the success of these programs and prevention activities is difficult to measure for several reasons, including that suicide is a complex event and data on suicides often lag by several years. Additionally, determining whether a death is intentional or unintentional, especially if the cause is drug overdose or a single-car collision, is difficult. Further, death certificates can contain inaccurate demographic information supplied by relatives or the funeral director (e.g., race or years of education) and do not include certain kinds of information (e.g., sexual orientation). Terms related to suicide may also not be part of cultural or religious lexicons. In these communities, data may not be collected or may be gathered differently. Some communities may be protective of their data because they are concerned about how the data might be used if shared or made public. Therefore, data might not be available or accurate.

Challenges for evaluation exist within health care environments as well. There is no systematic mapping and reconciling of different versions of suicide risk assessment instruments across health systems. There is no standard process for adequate suicide prevention follow-up care or procedures on how to evaluate effectiveness in different health systems with different care processes. And there is a lack of clarity in determining whether a safety-planning discussion took place between a clinician and patient or what that discussion entailed if there was one. Additionally, among suicide prevention programs in social service agencies, identifying meaningful program effects is difficult because many programs have multiple components, making it difficult to discern the components or characteristics responsible for any observed effect.

Suicide assessment measurement tools have problems of their own. Typically, these tools often are used inconsistently across studies, which makes comparisons impossible. In clinical environments, assessment tools are often single items; not used for non-suicide measures. For example, they might ask on an intake form, "Are you feeling suicidal? Yes or no." They are certainly not culturally or gender specific despite evidence that suicidal ideation and behaviors vary across groups. Finally, there are no accepted evaluation components across all suicide programs.

Evaluating Hotspots

There are several programs that include interventions proven to effectively reduce suicide at hotspots. These programs address the following: (a) restricting access to means (through installation of physical barriers); (b) increasing the likelihood of intervention by a third party (through surveillance and staff training); and (c) encouraging responsible media reporting of suicides (through guidelines for media professionals). The evidence also suggests that restricting access to means at one site does not drive suicidal individuals to seek alternative locations. The problem is not simply shifted elsewhere. There are also indications that reducing suicides by a particular method does not lead to substitution of different methods; instead, this action may have a positive impact on the overall suicide rate.[2]

The apparent effectiveness of installing barriers at suicide hotspots is consistent with the broader literature on restricting access to means as a population-level suicide prevention strategy, as discussed in Chapter 6. Reviews by Mann et al. (2005)[3] and Beautrais et al. (2007)[4] suggest that this form of restriction is one of few approaches with strong evidence of effectiveness.

Developing an Evaluation Plan

Despite the challenges in measuring the impact of suicide prevention activities, demonstrating impact to justify the services offered is crucial. More often than not, measurements of program outcome expectations come from various interested people or organizations often referred to as "stakeholders" and funders of the program (i.e., individual donors, foundations, or government) that want to ensure fiscal and service delivery accountability. Data are used to illustrate the problem, justify the need for an intervention, and measure the impact. Developing an evaluation

---

2   Cox et al. (2013). *BMC Public Health, 13*: 214, p. 9 of 12. http://www.biomed-central.com/1471-2458/13/214

3   Mann, J. J., Apter, A., Bertolote, J., Beautrais, A., et al. (2005). Suicide prevention strategies: A systematic review. *J Am Med Assoc, 294*(16): 2064–2074.

4   Beautrais, A., Fergusson, D., Coggan, C., Collings, C., et al. (2007). Effective strategies for suicide prevention in New Zealand: A review of the evidence. *NZ Med J, 120*(1251): U2459.

plan can help to clarify and guide the implementation of an evaluation approach. Important considerations include research questions, evaluation measures, evaluation design, and data-collection strategies.

Research Questions

The National Action Alliance for Suicide Prevention's Research Prioritization Task Force issued a prioritized research agenda in 2014, with the aim of more clearly defining the goals and mechanisms of research into suicide to move the field forward and lead to substantial reductions in suicides. The Suicide Research Prioritization Plan of Action[5] outlines the connections between the key questions, aspirational goals, research pathways, short-term objectives, and long-term objectives.

Aspirational research goals include the following:

1. Know what leads to or protects against suicidal behavior and learn how to change those things to prevent suicide.

2. Determine the degree of suicide risk (e.g., imminent, near-term, or long-term) among individuals in diverse populations and settings through feasible and effective screening and assessment approaches.

3. Predict who is at risk for suicide in the immediate future.

4. Ensure that people who are thinking about suicide but have not yet attempted it receive interventions to prevent suicidal behavior.

5. Find new biological treatments and better ways to use existing treatments to prevent suicidal behavior.

6. Ensure that people who have attempted suicide get effective interventions to prevent further attempts.

7. Ensure that health care providers and others in the community are well trained in how to find and treat those at risk.

8. Ensure that people at risk for suicidal behavior can access affordable care that works, no matter where they are.

---

5   The National Action Alliance for Suicide Prevention (Action Alliance). U.S. Department of Health and Human Services, Substance Abuse and Mental Health Services.

9. Ensure that people getting care for suicidal thoughts and behaviors are followed throughout their treatment so they don't fall through the cracks.

10. Increase help-seeking behaviors and referrals for at-risk individuals by decreasing stigma.

11. Prevent the emergence of suicidal behavior by developing and delivering the most effective prevention programs to build resilience and reduce risk in broad-based populations.

12. Reduce access to lethal means used to attempt suicide.

Specific research pathways for reducing access to lethal means are as follows:

- Examine changes in suicide risk as a result of policies that affect risk factors in the populations (e.g., reducing access to firearms for people at risk of suicide, improving monitoring of prescription medications to reduce overdose risk).

- Develop and test social messaging designed to increase the use and uptake of safety actions regarding lethal means (e.g., removal of guns from the home, use of gun locks, removal of lethal medications, and development of pedestrian-safe bridges) among at-risk individuals, family members, and community leaders in responsible positions. Community leaders may include gun club officials, campus staff, civil engineers, and heath care providers.

- Test approaches for safer prescribing so at-risk individuals receive medications with therapeutic value but less toxicity.

- Conduct research to assess how suicidal individuals seek, plan, and gain access to suicide means, including where and how this access can be disrupted through key points of contact (e.g., gun sellers, military commanders, and health care providers).

- Identify the individual, social, and ecological factors that influence public attitudes toward ways to reduce access to suicide means. Determine how these factors can effectively be used in traditional and social media campaigns, individual counseling, or both.

- Evaluate combinations of efforts such as social messaging, lethal means storage policies, and insurance policies on the impact of suicide prevention.

- Determine the most efficient ways of delivering means safety messaging and access to crisis counseling by those who help at-risk people outside the health care setting (e.g., ministers, lawyers, gun shop owners, or college counselors/faculty/peers.

Evaluation Design

According to the RAND Suicide Prevention Program Evaluation Toolkit, the five most common types of evaluation designs used in evaluating suicide prevention programs, listed from most to least rigorous, are as follows:

1. Pre-/post-intervention evaluation with a control group. This type of evaluation requires you to randomly assign your pool of program participants to either participate in the program (intervention group) or not participate in the program (control group) and collect data at two time points—before the program starts and after the program ends.

2. Pre-/post-intervention evaluation with a comparison group. This evaluation is the same as number 4 below except you also collect data from a group that did not participate in the program but is similar in composition to the participating group.

3. Interrupted time-series analysis. This approach uses secondary data (i.e., census data or school data) to assess changes at multiple time points before and after the program.

4. Pre-/post-intervention evaluation. This type of evaluation involves collecting data from program participants at two time points: before the program starts and after the program ends.

5. Retrospective pre-/post-intervention evaluation. This type of evaluation involves collecting data from program participants at only one time point but asking them how their skills, knowledge, or behaviors have changed since before the program.[6]

---

6   RAND Suicide Prevention Program Evaluation Toolkit 52.

Data Collection Strategies

Data tell you the who, what, and how of suicide in your area. Using national and local data to pinpoint high suicide death and attempt rates by age, gender, ethnicity, and life circumstance (e.g., veteran status) can help you decide where to focus your efforts and choose appropriate strategies. Data on related risk and protective factors, such as substance abuse and violence, can also help you better target your prevention efforts.[7] This information is critical when seeking funding, and it helps keep your current supporters energized. If suicide data about a local subgroup of interest (e.g., ethnic communities or age groups) are not available, look for national data on the group, then consult general data about suicides in your area.

To get an even clearer sense of the suicide problem in your community, you can build partnerships to access other data sources or work with partner organizations to create a system for collecting new information. Other more informal data sources, such as needs assessments, stakeholder interviews (interested people or organizations), and focus groups, can supplement surveillance data and inform questions asked in quantitative instruments.

Commonly used national sources of data for information on suicide deaths include the following:

- The CDC's National Vital Statistics System: annual data on all suicide deaths occurring in the United States; available from WISQARS (www.cdc.gov/injury/wisqars);

- CDC's NVDRS: annual data on suicide deaths from 18 states; available from WISQARS (www.cdc.gov/injury/wisqars/nvdrs.html);

- The CDC's Youth Risk Behavior Surveillance System: data released every 2 years on suicide ideation and attempts among high school students (www.cdc.gov/healthyyouth/yrbs/index.htm);

- SAMHSA's National Survey on Drug Use and Health: annual survey that, since 2008, has included questions on suicidal thoughts and behaviors among adults (www.oas.samhsa.gov/nsduh.htm); and

---

7   Suicide Prevention Resource Center. (2020). Core competency: Data and surveillance. https://www.sprc.org/grantees/core-competencies/data

▪ Wide-ranging Online Data for Epidemiologic Research (WONDER) (https://healthdata.gov/dataset/wide-ranging-online-data-epidemiologic-research-wonder).

Evaluation of Efforts

When evaluating traditional suicide prevention programs, the process is generally straightforward and often laid out ahead of time if a funding grant proposal is involved. The process includes developing a research team, involving stakeholders, developing a logic model with specific, measurable, attainable, relevant, and time-based (SMART) goals. Continuous analysis in the form of process and outcome evaluation is critical to demonstrate impact. However, community organizing efforts frequently require long time frames to come to fruition. The process of growing and mobilizing a base, building support, shifting attitudes and changes, policies, or practices does not happen overnight. Holding those in power accountable for the change also takes time. As we have seen with the Golden Gate, organizing to reduce access to lethal means can be complex and iterative. Strategies shift based on the external environment and outcomes are not readily quantifiable. However, that does not mean that it does not need to be accountable for monitoring progress and outcomes.

A community organizing evaluation is effective when it involves the participants in an ongoing and meaningful way. This approach leverages strengths and learning through the process rather than judgment or pass/fail accountability. It allows for real-time data collection and feedback from community members. The receptivity enables them to work in greater partnership and credit achievement for leadership development and capacity development goals.

Logic Model

The Composite Logic Model developed by the Aspen Institute can be used to help advocates, funders, and evaluators articulate an advocacy or policy change strategy or theory of change. There is both a paper and a web-based version of the model. The web version, Advocacy Progress Planner (APP), developed by the Aspen Institute's Continuous Progress Strategic Services,[8] allows advocates to see the effects of their planned

---

8   Aspen Institute, The Composite Logic Model. Copyright © by Aspen Institute.

campaign as it develops and to revise and improve it. The composite logic model can be used to help advocates, funders, and evaluators articulate an advocacy or policy change strategy.[9]

The eight questions below guide users on how to use the model for that purpose:

1. What is the advocacy or policy change goal?

   Start by defining what, in the end, the advocacy strategy is trying to achieve … Or the policy may already exist, and the goal is making sure it is implemented correctly and is having its intended impact.

   In the case of suicide prevention, the goal is developing a solution and getting that solution adopted as policy.

2. Who is the audience?

   Select the audience(s) that the strategy needs to reach to achieve its goal(s). Think both about who needs to be part of the advocacy effort and which decision makers need to be convinced in order to achieve the strategy's goal. Most strategies will target multiple audiences.

3. What will it take to convince or move the audience?

   Consider the *inputs*, activities, and *interim outcomes* in the composite logic model. What do those involved in the advocacy or policy change effort need to do to move the strategy's audience and achieve its goal?

4. What contextual factors might affect the strategy's success?

   Think about the factors that are not controllable but that may impact the strategy's success and therefore are important to keep in mind.

5. Where doesn't the strategy need to focus?

   Consider whether there are *inputs, activities, and outcomes* on the model that are already in place and either don't have to be built (but can be leveraged) or are not relevant to the strategy. For example, among the interim outcomes, awareness about an issue

---

9   Using the Composite Logic Model to Articulate an Advocacy Strategy or Theory of Change. http://www.pointk.org/client_docs/File/advocacy/clm_questions.pdf

or problem may already be high and therefore not a focus; the challenge instead will be increasing the audience's perception of its salience.

6. What will strategy collaborators do?

One advantage of the composite logic model is that it identifies a full range of possible advocacy activities and outcomes. As a result, it can be used to identify where other organizations or collaborators are positioned and how they complement the strategy. Identifying collaborators' positioning puts the strategy in context and shows where and how it will add value. It also illustrates potential points of synergy and collaboration that might not already exist.

7. What will the opposition or competition do?

Think about how the opposition is positioned. Consider whether counteractions are necessary, particularly where there is activity or outcome overlap. For example, if the opposition has a media strategy, consider potential audience reactions to competing messages and how to frame messages accordingly.

8. Is there a contingency plan?

If relevant, identify alternative paths to the end goal if the current strategy is not successful. Consider which components in the model will signal if the strategy is not working. For example, if the strategy is not successful in generating policy maker champions using one-on-one briefings with those policy makers, it may be necessary to build a larger cadre of advocates at the local level who will demonstrate demand and make a grassroots case for change.

Benchmarks

Unlike mental health programs, it is not feasible to institute validated assessment tools to demonstrate the effectiveness of restricting access to lethal means. However, benchmarks can be identified to be indicative of impact. Examples of benchmarks include:

- Changes in numbers, demographics, location, and numbers;
- Changes in attitudes, skills, and knowledge;

- Establishment of relationships/changes in stature within community or among decision makers;
- Changes in group membership;
- Changes in participation to group events;
- Policy success;
- Shifts in norms or content of debate;
- Policy implementation;
- Shifts in practices;
- Public accountability for inaction;
- Documented impact on community;
- Changes in staffing, infrastructure, skills, or resources; and
- Changing systems to accurately capture data and using it to refine strategy.

Data Collection

Methods for data collection beyond tracking morbidity and mortality can include the following:

- Membership and attendance tracking;
- Interviews and focus groups;
- Tracking elements of leadership growth;
- Relationship/champion tracking;
- Base-building tracking;
- Media tracking;
- Policy development tracking;
- Interviews;
- Review of public records;
- Collection of archival documents; and
- Organizational capacity assessment.

Sharing Results

Sharing evaluation findings is a strategy for communicating the value of a suicide prevention program, marketing the program to other groups and individuals, securing more funding, and influencing policy decisions. Consider the following when developing a plan for sharing evaluation results:[10]

- **Coordinate with stakeholders:** Ensure evaluation findings meet the needs of stakeholders by involving them in the review and discussion of results.

- **Create a communications plan:** Identify techniques for conveying results, such as short videos, newsletters, audio segments, websites, or presentations to community partners or other groups.

- **Consider the audience:** Ensure the evaluation results are clear, concise, and appropriately formatted for different audiences.

- **Describe important features of the program and evaluation:** Share contextual information for the evaluation, including background and purpose, methods, findings, conclusions, recommendations, and lessons learned.

- **Present meaningful information effectively:** Use graphics, charts, and tables to present data. Include examples and meaningful anecdotal narratives. Avoid technical jargon and acronyms in writing.

- **Be upfront about the strengths and limitations:** List the strengths and limitations of the evaluation. Discuss the advantages and disadvantages of the results and recommendations.

Timeliness matters and providing real-time data is often challenging because it is difficult to propagate learning in ongoing, sensitive campaigns. The politics and complex communications paths in coalitions can slow down or complicate information sharing. It is important to be patient, focused, as transparent as possible, and to provide analysis in an accessible way.

---

10   The Columbia Lighthouse Project. (2016). The Colombia-Suicide Severity Rating Scale (C-SSRS). http://cssrs.columbia.edu/

Image Credits

8

Projects in Organizing for Suicide Prevention

Central to the theme of this book is the idea that organized groups of advocates can address suicide hotspots in their own community. By extension, we believe this can apply to other concerns in mental health, housing, and other areas. As a means to consider how such activity might be launched in your community, we have developed a set of exercises to assist you in launching and sustaining an advocacy program. The exercises below follow the chapter structure of this book. Naturally, it is not possible for a developing advocacy campaign to address every point that follows. However, we believe knowing what points might be addressed allows advocates to select the most important and relevant and apply those in the specific situation they confront.

EXERCISE: ASSESS THE SITUATION

▷ Determine if a "hotspot" or similar problem exists in your community. What is the local prevalence and incidence of suicide? Determine who maintains the data. If it is uncommon for the epidemiology to be systematically maintained, identify the entities, such as coroner, port commissioner, local police, and highway patrol, who might have relevant data. Please note that there may be multiple entities that maintain their own data, and it may be conflicting.

▷ Evaluate the use of media reporting for the frequency, content of messaging, and tone of the story. Is there transparency? Are there specific reporters who seem to be championing the issue? If the information is not formally disseminated, consider informal information methods like social media that captures suicide attempts and/or completions at particular sites. Are media guidelines for responsible reporting of suicides followed?[1]

▷ Are there vocal individuals addressing the issue? Survivors? Family members? Skeptics? What is the action that they are calling for? Increased mental health services, early detection, training, reducing access to lethal means?

▷ Who are the survivors (individual survivors, surviving family members, and community members) who have been personally impacted? Have they been vocal about their experiences, and if so, how?

▷ Is there a county- or city-wide suicide prevention strategic plan in place, and does it include access to lethal means restriction? Identify the local suicide prevention organizations and public health activists.

▷ Identify what existing suicide prevention programs exist in the impacted community. Are there accessible hotline phones or numbers posted? Are community nonprofits, hospital systems, or community public health campaigns engaged in suicide prevention? Are there local physician or psychiatric service providers who are or would like the opportunity to be vocal about the problem?

▷ Have there been previous efforts to address the problem at the particular hotspot, and if so, by whom? What were the setbacks? Articulate the narrative of prevention efforts. Consider the problems created by the dissemination of false information about the effectiveness of limiting access to lethal means.

---

[1] American Foundation for Suicide Prevention Media Guidelines: https://afsp.org/wp-content/uploads/2016/01/recommendations.pdf

▷ Identify who "owns" the hotspot. Who has legal and financial responsibility for the hotspot's maintenance and safety? Who makes the decisions about the expenditures related to construction? If there is a board of directors for an existing organization, is it diverse and representative of all stakeholders, including family survivors?

▷ Write a narrative describing the history of the hotspot and the challenges and previous attempts to address the problem and potential challenges an advocate might face.

FIGURE 8.1 Kevin Hines, who survived a jump from the bridge, surveys the *Whose Shoes?* exhibit, commemorating lives lost at the Golden Gate.

EXERCISE: EVALUATE AND POSITION WITHIN THE LARGER LANDSCAPE

▷ What is the rate of suicide in your target community, and how does it compare to the national and state averages? Find comparison data at https://www.cdc.gov/nchs/pressroom/sosmap/suicide-mortality/suicide.htm

▷ What was the most prevalent mechanism of injury? What were the rates compared with other geographic areas? Use WISQARS® Fatal

Mapping Module to generate geospatially smoothed, age-adjusted suicide death rates by county. See https://www.cdc.gov/injury/wisqars/WISQARS-Mapping-Module.html

▷ What are the demographics of suicide in your target community? Consider age, race and ethnicity, gender, LGBT status, and military and veteran status. Consider referencing state and county health department data and information from coroners or medical examiners.

▷ If epidemiological data does not exist, reference the World Health Organization public health surveillance system for suicide attempts and self-harm cases presenting to general hospitals based on medical record.

▷ What are the annualized estimates of the total lifetime medical and work-loss costs?

EXERCISE: ORGANIZE

▷ Who has access to local prevalence and incidence data? Do laws or policies support the reporting of the data at regular intervals? If no, consider convening individuals who have access, such as coroners, first responders, and Coast Guard. Operationalize terms and develop systems for systematically capturing and reporting data.

▷ If there were reports of suicide by the media of notable circumstances (i.e., women, youth, veterans, etc.), how did the community respond?

▷ From your list of groups working on addressing this issue, do they adequately represent all those impacted or concerned?

▷ List other groups and constituents who may be interested in the issue but have not yet engaged. Keep in mind that they might not have felt valued or invited to come to the table.

▷ Determine if the conversations among those with decision-making authority are transparent. If not, determine what can be done from a policy perspective to mandate transparency. Consider open meetings, minute taking, public records, and video access to meetings.

▷ Critique the work the decision makers are doing. Describe their position and the actions they have taken. Assess their individual and collective levels of motivation in solving the problem.[2]

▷ Identify and understand the nature of opposition. For those addressing suicides on bridges, is there a poor understanding of suicide and suicide prevention, fear of a negative impact on the structure's aesthetics, or concern about the cost of construction, or the impact on tourism?

▷ Determine how you can build further awareness and motivation.

   1. Consider using film, such as a documentary, or printed articles, publishing demographics of victims;

   2. Train survivors or family survivors of loss on public speaking;

   3. Develop visual renderings of barriers that could be created. Student groups can be a great source of free labor, which has a mutual benefit; and

   4. Request that local physicians and psychiatric societies publish op-eds on suicide and the effectiveness of means restriction.

▷ Propose a public event that will help tell your story and describe how it will provide both important background to understanding the issue and a strong visual appearance attractive to video and still photography.

▷ How would you structure an organization or coalition to address the issue? Will it be an independent nonprofit, or will an existing organization sponsor it? What funds will it need to operate? Who will lead the organization? Do they demonstrate flexibility and inclusiveness in their leadership style?

---

2   Prochaska & DiClemente, 1983; Prochaska, DiClemente, & Norcross, 1992.

FIGURE 8.2 The Golden Gate from Baker Beach, where every year families who have suffered a suicide loss at the bridge gather to remember and write the names of lost loved ones in the sand.

EXERCISE: COMMUNICATE

▷ Identify a forum for regular communication of the problem. Consider use of existing social media and the development of a new website. Publish and speak publicly about the research (formally in print or informally on blogs), citing the effectiveness about reducing access to lethal means.

▷ Prepare an annotated list of peer-reviewed published research and talking points that discuss or provide insight into the problem you seek to remedy.

▷ Summarize that research in a document you can share with the press.

▷ Develop a communication strategy for the general public to ensure the issues stay in their consciousness.

▷ If you are advocating a project that involves construction, provide a detailed rendering of what the proposed project is. Recruit support from volunteer professionals or at local schools of engineering or architecture in your area.

▷ Identify families and friends of suicide loss who are willing to tell their stories. Provide training on public speaking and storytelling to elicit change. Develop a schedule for a timely response to suicides when they occur.

▷ Solicit input and interest in the writing of regular publications from within the professional mental health (psychiatric) and volunteer advocate community.

▷ Identify media outlets (local and national) that might be interested in regular stories about the problem hotspot. Develop a coordinated plan for responding to news of suicide attempts and deaths. Develop a background media kit with relevant data and the suicide reporting guidelines and contact information for your advocacy group.

▷ Outline a social media strategy to communicate with the general public, identified supporters, and other interested parties.

EXERCISE: ENGAGE DECISION MAKERS

▷ Describe what "enraged constituents" might mean in a practical sense. What are the strengths and weaknesses of organizations with such constituents? List examples from other advocacy programs and cite references to support your arguments.

▷ Considering the suicide problem, other issue, or location you identified earlier, list three action items you might recommend that would both address the issue before the public and further encourage—or strengthen the resolve of—your volunteer advocates. Consider putting processes in place to obtain and tell their stories of loss and survival.

▷ Develop the stories that might create presentations, news events, or public interest in your advocacy. Circulate petitions and similar means to encourage involvement.

▷ Identify elected leaders who might champion the cause. Describe how you might work with these individuals and make best use of the authority they have. Consider providing them with talking points and a summary of the relevant research and evidence of the efficacy of barriers.

▷ Research state and federal laws in your area that may assist in your advocacy work. Include consideration of public record access, transportation safety, and disability rights and other areas. Is there specific language for transportation funds to use for safety or even life-saving safety barriers or nets?

▷ Include advocates in the design review process.

EXERCISE: EXPLORE PREVENTION EFFORTS

▷ Does a local strategic suicide prevention plan exist that incorporates the National Strategy? Does it identify and address the issues you have identified?

▷ What are the local behavioral health programs that exist in the community surrounding the hotspot? Do they address primary, secondary, and tertiary behavioral interventions? Where are the gaps? Are they collaboratively engaged in reducing the prevalence of suicide?

▷ Among the social service programs that exist in your community, which incorporate recommendations from the SPRC National Strategy? How do these programs do so? Where are the gaps?

▷ Describe 10 representations of suicide in popular culture—from history or fiction—and discuss how they are presented. What prevention options are open to the suicidal character in the story?

▷ How are misconceptions about suicide expressed in your community?

EXERCISE: ADDRESS MISCONCEPTIONS AND THE UTILIZATION OF EVIDENCE-BASED INTERVENTIONS

▷ Conduct research on suicides in your area. Check the National Violent Death Reporting System, look carefully at medical records, and talk to family members of the victims to determine if there was a previously diagnosed mental health condition.[3]

▷ Although it may be tempting, do not inflate the numbers in your reports; ensure your data is always accurate and reliable.

▷ Conduct a cultural profile of your community. Use census or other data county to identify the racial, ethnic, linguistic, and socioeconomic demographics of your community. Based on the results, research culturally specific attitudes on suicide.

▷ Use county public health data to determine the prevalence and incidences of mental health diagnoses. If you have access to geo-mapping, identify areas of high risk/need and their proximity to suicide hotspots.

▷ Determine which (if any) suicide prevention techniques are being used in your community. Consider media coverage, general public education, screening, gatekeeper training, primary care physician education, counseling, and means restriction.

▷ Ensure that community members are aware of the revised National Strategy for Suicide Prevention 2001. Conduct public forums to highlight recommendations and solicit feedback.

▷ Evaluate community members' knowledge about empirical evidence with regard to means restriction. This can be accomplished formally through surveys and/or informally through peer interaction. Maintain field notes or a journal to record your observations.

---

3   National Center for Injury Prevention and Control, Division of Violence Prevention. (2019, Nov. 7). National Violent Death Reporting System (NVDRS). Center for Disease Control and Prevention. https://www.cdc.gov/violenceprevention/datasources/nvdrs/index.html?CDC_AA_refVal=https%3A%2F%2Fwww.cdc.gov%2Fviolenceprevention%2Fnvdrs%2Findex.html

Note tangible comments and intangible tone of responses about the subject, especially related to the substitution fallacy.

EXERCISE: EVALUATE PROGRESS

▷ If partnered with a university and conducting behavioral research on suicide prevention, develop a research team, involve stakeholders, develop a logic model with specific, measurable, attainable, relevant, and time-based (SMART) goals, and continuously analyze in the form of process and outcome evaluation in order to demonstrate impact.

▷ To evaluate community organizing and advocacy, clearly restate your goals and objectives regarding target populations, anticipated reach, social media platforms, and expected outcomes. List benchmarks and the steps needed for approval of the solution you propose.

▷ Use the Advocacy Progress Planner (APP), developed by the Aspen Institute's Continuous Progress Strategic Services, which allows advocates to see the effects of their planned campaign as it develops and to revise and improve it: http://www.planning. continuousprogress.org.

▷ Use multiple methods to evaluate progress toward your goal by soliciting regular feedback from participants and community members. Consider including interviews, focus groups, hits on websites, published stories and opinion pieces, and social media followers.

▷ Conduct surveys at large-scale events to gather data to analyze campaign reach and effectiveness. Use pretest and posttest assessments of community perception and knowledge to evaluate reach and comprehension of your campaign.

▷ Regularly review data on related factors and health issues (e.g., substance abuse or violence) and incorporate them into program planning.

▷ Communicate important data to stakeholders to sustain their support, ensuring that they are apprised of all milestones and setbacks.

FIGURE 8.3 Approved! Supporters gather in the stairway outside the Bridge District boardroom after the district vote to approve a construction contract for the suicide deterrent net.

Image Credits

Fig. 8.1: Copyright © 2012 Bridge Rail Foundation/Cristina Taccone. Reprinted with permission.

Fig. 8.2: Copyright © 2010 by Bridge Rail Foundation. Reprinted with permission.

Fig. 8.3: Copyright © 2016 by Bridge Rail Foundation. Reprinted with permission.

INDEX